THE WAY OF A COUNTRYMAN

IAN NIALL

Illustrations by C.F. TUNNICLIFFE

Foreword by BERNARD O'DONOGHUE

This edition published by Merlin Unwin Books, 2012

First published in 1965 by Country Life Ltd
Published in 1993 by White Lion Books
Reprinted 1996, 2000

ISBN 978-1-906122-46-1

British Library Cataloguing-in-Publication Data
A catalogue record for this book is available from the British
Library

Merlin Unwin Books
Palmers House
7 Corve Street
Ludlow
Shropshire SY8 1DB
www.merlinunwin.co.uk

Printed and bound in England by Jellyfish Print Solutions

CONTENTS

IAN NIALL (1916-2002) was the pen name of John McNeillie, author of over forty books on country matters. In 1990 he celebrated forty years as a columnist, at one point both for *The Spectator* and for *Country Life* where he was known and loved by a wide public for his weekly 'Countryman's Notes'. He was born in Scotland and he spent his formative years on his grandfather's farm in Wigtownshire, recalled in *A Galloway Childhood*. He and his wife then lived in Wales and, later, the Chilterns. They had three children. His son Andrew McNeillie, Professor Emeritus at Exeter University, runs the Clutag Press and is the author of a biographical memoir of his father, *Ian Niall: Part of his Life*.

CHARLES TUNNICLIFFE (1901-1979) was raised on a small farm in Cheshire. He was expected to take over his father's smallholding, but his precocious talent as an artist set him apart and in 1920 he took a scholarship to the Royal College of Art. Tunnicliffe soon made his mark as an etcher and wood-engraver and in 1932 came his first major success with his illustrated edition of *Tarka the Otter* by Henry Williamson. He went on to illustrate dozens of books for well-known authors. He also produced several classic books of his own including his masterpiece *Shorelands Summer Diary*. Had Tunnicliffe done nothing other than illustrate books, his name would be remembered. But his achievement as a wildlife artist, and in particular a bird artist, is of major importance. Turning to the study of birds in the 1930s, he spent long hours observing and sketching his favourite species, first on the Cheshire meres and nearby moors, then in Anglesey, his home from 1947 until his death in 1979.

BERNARD O'DONOGHUE was born in Cullen in the rural depths of North Cork in 1945. He moved to Manchester in 1962 and since 1965 has lived in Oxford where he is now an Emeritus Fellow of Wadham College. He has published several books of poetry including: *Gunpowder* (1995), a choice of the Poetry Society and winner of the Whitbread poetry prize, and most recently *Farmers Cross*. His wife Heather is a scholar of Old Norse; they have three children.

FOREWORD

by Bernard O' Donoghue

In his poem 'A Daylight Art' dedicated to the lucid Scottish poet Norman MacCaig, Seamus Heaney reaches a Horatian conclusion about art:

> Happy the man, therefore, with a natural gift for practising
> the right one from the start – poetry, say, or fishing.

Ian Niall can claim this happiness. Although his feel for poetic expression is evident in every line of his writing, it is fowling that vies with fishing as his instinctively right art. And instinct is the essential faculty of the countryman in Niall's book, an instinct shared with the animals with which the world is shared.

The temper of the book is a rare blend of epigrammatic classicism with a controlled romantic nostalgia. From the opening chapter's eloquent threnody for the corncrake to the days cutting turf (as we would term it in Ireland) on Clanty Moss, to the severe closing insistence on ethical responsibility in the exercise of the hunter's art, this is a grown-up's nature book, with all the pleasures remembered from the childhood books that introduced us to nature writing.

Ian Niall is full of wonderful epigrams to express the mystery of his countryman's instinct for nature: 'his eye was better than his eyesight', for example. With modest reluctance the writer claims this extra-sensory perception for himself in his fishing chapter, 'About With a Rod'. To the layperson it is familiar in a lesser form as the lateral thinking with which all practitioners of sport are familiar: 'on a good day I have fished for hours without success convinced that I would come to the moment when I would begin to do well. On a bad day I have known that I was doomed to fish without success until I put the rod away again.'

The mystical impulse is best represented in this lyrical book by its animal legends and narratives: the folk-belief in the woodcock's ability to splint its own leg; the poetic view of the farmer on Ty Newydd (haunting for the declining number of us who were kept awake by the craking in hot childhood summers) that the corncrake 'had simply gone silent; it was a secret bird; it had always been of that habit'; or the village riot provoked by the fox which recalls Chaucer's *Nun's Priest's Tale*: 'the fox has a natural bent for mischief, a sort of recklessness that suddenly puts him out in the open in the middle of the day with the whole village gasping and pointing and scrambling for weapons, releasing penned dogs, plundering for an old gun and a cartridge.' The most haunting passage in the book describes the pathos of 'geese conversations' when the fat domestic geese call out in reply to the migratory wild geese fleeing south before the threats of the coming winter. With a twinkling sideswipe, Niall reflects that these poor fattened creatures are 'no more equipped to join the flight than a portly stockbroker is equipped to hunt the mountain for his food'. But what Niall calls the 'primitive and primeval instincts' with which that scene is witnessed take the reader back to the rich harshness of the Old English elegies.

It is hard to stop comparing Ian Niall to the major landmarks of the literature. Maybe the most apt comparison is with the comment by the American critic Edmund Wilson who complained of John Steinbeck that he did not appreciate the difference between human beings and animals. This is a criticism, I suspect, that Niall would take as a compliment. In his world, man's instinct is a poor relation to that of animals; but he must go on trying. And he must attempt to emulate nature according to the rules. The two great passions of this book are aesthetic and ethical: things must be done right, and they must be done justly. In the book's powerful nostalgic conclusion 'Looking Both Ways' the moral is stated firmly: 'it befits the serious shooting man to see that what is best in sporting ethics is passed on and what is reprehensible is put away.' The 'shooting man' is as serious as anyone else in the pursuit of his art, and no less subject to ethical rule. Niall never patronises his subject. He doesn't even patronise his gun, as he stares at it with an unwavering craftsman's eye: 'the chasing on sidelocks, the rampant hammers as graceful in shape as anything in nature'.

This appreciative eye is wonderfully served by the illustrations by C.F. Tunnicliffe. These illustrations are the sealing distinction of a perfectly executed book. Tunnicliffe is, I suppose, the greatest English representational nature artist of his time. The clean precision of Niall's writing is precisely matched by Tunnicliffe's perfectionism: witness his lurking pike, his snipe banking, the unctuous innocence of his partridge. There is a perfect matching of skills here; both artists achieve a wistful celebration of their world through a classical fidelity which is proof against sentimentality. If this book really is an elegy for a world which is past or passing, it offers the consolation of an unforgettable panegyric.

Bernard O'Donoghue
Oxford

INTRODUCTION

THE recollections of a man whose greatest delight has been in the things he found in the open air are always dotted with small, almost insignificant things that were the mortar of his experience. With every countryman, sportsman, naturalist, these things are different. My own recollections are never significant in that I can speak of the day when I landed a specimen trout, twice performed the feat of a left and right at woodcock or witnessed the mating of eagles. These things never came my way, although I yet have hopes of the trout. Yesterday, it seems, I watched and listened to the corncrake. Not so long ago I took my best trout from a wild mountain lake, but there was also the day when I couldn't stop catching pike, when I slipped and damaged my old Damascus barrelled gun (it had been given me by my grandfather) and removed the dent with the cleaning gear and some tow, when I unearthed the hedgehog's litter and took two home to make pets of them.

I was born with the hunter's instinct. Nothing has fascinated me more than guns, the smell of powder, the half-cock and cocking click of an old fowling piece, the chasing on sidelocks, the rampant hammers as graceful in shape as anything in nature, the beauty of a walnut stock inset with silver, or the utilitarian solidness of guns designed for youthful scarecrows and pothunters. To handle old guns stimulated me as a boy. I looked ahead to days in the bog fields, the water meadows, the woods and stubbles. I had great dreams not of slaughter, but a hunter's dreams. Now when I handle these same old guns my mind conjures things I shall never see – the bustard on the plains, Colonel Hawker trying the percussion-cap muzzle-loaders that were new in his day, remote and secret marshes where the fowlers took their birds with ancient guns and devices no one today would know how to use.

Among my recollections are accounts handed down to me by my grandfather, whose first enterprise in life was to persuade two farmers to engage him to kill birds on their adjoining barley fields, one providing the shot and the other the powder, leaving their youthful bird-scarer to sell what he could shoot. How I wished that I could have stepped back with him to perch in the tree, prime the gun and take the fabulous shots he took to bag more pigeons than a small cart could carry. My father, too, was a man born with a love of the field such as every man that walks once had, even if most townsmen have been conditioned to their environment. I walked with both my grandfather and my father learning the ways of the wood and of nature and if I stood at the gate again I would walk no other way, nor would I want to.

PARTRIDGES AND CRAKES

◇◇◇

IN the spring, when I was a child, the increasing brightness of the cold days of February and March meant that soon the horses would be unhitched from the ploughs and set to pulling the harrows on the land to be seeded with oats. The peewit nests in March and April, but in those days the progress of agriculture was such that not every field was harrowed and rolled before the sea pie and plover brought off her young. The chicks of ground birds, which the oyster-catcher can hardly be called since its proper place is the shore, were able to save themselves, for, like the young of the waterhen, nature has equipped them for the emergency. They can run almost from the time their down is dry, just as the waterhen's chicks are able to swim when the water rises to flood their nest.

We regularly had the eggs of the peewit for breakfast. Sometimes the curlew's eggs were taken and the nest of the waterhen was milked of one or two. Country folk had as much appreciation of a delicacy as any gourmet. On Sundays, while their masters went off to church in their gigs, with harness shining and brass all burnished, the ploughman, and most farm boys, wandered the brown fields searching for the nests of the peewit. In the first week of April there was something wrong if an hour or two of wandering didn't produce at least two or three dozen eggs. Not every collector's gathering went to the kitchen, of course. Some wrapped the eggs in fragments of newspaper and packed them in a stout box to send them off to London where they were sold at extortionate prices to people who had never seen the bird, or breathed the cold spring air on a ploughed field in April.

Egg-collectors of other sorts there were, but most harvested the peewit's eggs knowing that in any case the harrows would rip through every nest before the field was ready for rolling. They could tell the fresh egg from the one that was incubated without going to the ditch to see whether it floated or not. The texture of the shell was different; the shine was identification enough, but the feel confirmed it all. It was inevitable that these egg-gatherers should meet now and then and that their rivalry result in sabotage on occasions. Many of them carried their eggs in their caps, which they wore on their heads, and the less agile ploughboy often found himself with shell and yolk trickling through his hair after he had been jostled and ordered to find some new place to search. When the partridges began to haunt the banks and the grass rose to give shelter to the corncrake, all this activity ceased. No one robbed the partridge. Few could find the 'crake's nest and to trample the hay was something no farmer would permit, even if he thought nothing of birds. Looking back and considering the rarity of the 'crake at the present time, I am inclined to think that although it was common – I have heard five or six birds calling from adjoining fields in one evening – it was already doomed when I was a boy. A hundred years before it must have been common almost everywhere. My grandmother had been known to complain that the sound of the 'crake was tiresome and she, good solid countrywoman that she was, didn't suffer from nerves.

We lived in a part of the country to which the latest inventions permeated slowly. Farming methods were old-fashioned by standards elsewhere. There were still as many tilting reapers in the corn as there were binders and although most farmers had hay reapers it was not unknown for two or three mowers to be given a five-acre field of ryegrass to cut. Bog hay was always scythed. The 'crakes had time to incubate and lead their young away while the mowers swung and lurched their way into the long grass. Even the hay reaper would bog down and choke its knives in some fields. The corncrakes stalked through the forest of fine grass without great alarm. They brought off their broods and led them to safety and they came again, summer after summer, until the reaping machines were improved and men who could mow with scythes went to their long rest.

My grandfather had been the only man in his part of the world who fully understood the mechanism of the corn binder. The binder had been in use elsewhere, but in our undulating, stony ground with its protruding rocks people had been reluctant to change. When the new-fangled machines broke down someone with an understanding of the parts of a twine-knotter had to be on hand; someone who could straighten a shaft or see why the sheaves bundled up and were not ejected. As soon as the knowledge of these things became general a revolution began to take place both in the cornfield and the hayfield. The merits of one sort of harvesting machine against those of another

3

were critically judged. The blacksmiths and farmers were keen to take the heartbreak out of harvest. They were also banishing the 'crakes from the meadow. Not everywhere did the new green or red painted monsters appear at once. Not every farmer had the capital to invest. Here and there a smallholder, a crofter, worked his stony ground with ancient tools and out-of-date methods because he hadn't a penny with which to bless himself.

The corncrake still called from the fringe of the arable country, from little, hidden-away paddocks where the rising hay was dotted with yellow-flowered weeds and seeding thistles. In such places a man would still wade into his meagre crop of hay with a scythe in his hands and a sharpening stone in his hip pocket. The sound of the stone on the blade while the sun rode the summer sky kept the 'crakes silent, but at evening they called again. Only in such places did they survive. In a decade people who had been unconscious of the sounds of summer pricked up their ears and said: 'Do you know, I hear a corncrake.' Once the corncrake had been as much a part of the summer's day as the buzzing of the bee in the clover, the purring of turtle doves among the trees at the wood's edge. When I was quite small the magic in finding a peewit's nest was something I can't even yet describe. There is surely nothing more beautiful than the sight of four pointed, delicately coloured, marled and blotched eggs that blend so well with their surroundings that if you look away for an instant you must look carefully a second time to spot them from any appreciable distance. The peewits would run and then sail into the air crying, the whole business being designed to mislead a watcher. The partridge and the corncrake relied more on furtive, unobtrusive movement to make their get-away. The nests of both could be hard to find until the exact area could be marked with certainty. I began to search for the nests of both birds when I was barely big enough to be allowed to wander abroad in the fields alone. Having seen a pan basket taken to gather peewit eggs I took a great basket to bring back the eggs of the partridges and corncrakes I might find!

There was no chance that I might come home with a basket of corncrake's eggs, of course. The corncrake nested in the long grass on the shoulder of a hill leading down to the stream, or away out in a feathery patch of ryegrass, an island in the bog field of round rushes, and to find the nest required skill I hadn't yet developed. The art of finding the nest of a bird is something that is cultivated in childhood when the eyesight is keen and every sense alert, but ground birds, too, have their own ways of misleading the searcher, and the corncrake, like the water rail, is a master of tactics, of moving and making a short, misleading flight and subtly leading its enemy astray. The corncrake, I have sometimes thought, has the power of the expert ventriloquist. The partridge is less secretive, but it, too, knows the way to lure a searcher on and trails a wing, stands on a knoll and makes a short flight until it judges it may safely make a longer one.

I had discovered, however, that a certain track up the side of a hill had a great attraction for the nesting partridges. Along one stretch of drystone wall and gorse and blackberry hedge three or four birds might be seen at different times on a spring day and, sooner or later, there would be those little runs and rushes that mating birds make and it was plain that they were nesting in the cover of the gorse and bramble. How many eggs does a partridge lay? It depends, but at least a dozen may be found, and often many more. I carried the basket and came back with more than forty eggs. I was very happy to think that there would be a fine feast as a result of my egg-gathering, but how bitter was my disillusionment! What horror was shown when I came into the steading, and back I was marched to replace the eggs in the nests I had robbed! Never, never again was I to think of such a

thing. It was a crime. It was wicked. I was to think on the fact
that already I had probably caused four partridges to desert their
nests. Everyone loved the little birds. They were game, but they
were loved and I would see them taking a dust bath on the turnip
field or running through the rows when the potatoes were lifted
or leading their broods across the paddock to pick insects under
the beehives. Not only was I forbidden to take their eggs, I was
forbidden to go near the hedge in which they nested. It was
hard to understand why the partridge was sacred and the plover
plundered of her eggs.

It is no use pretending that I didn't look for the nest of both
the partridge and the corncrake, for I did, trampling down much
young grass and standing hay before I found the 'crake's eggs.
When I found them I was as delighted as I had been when in an
earlier summer I had found the eggs of the night jar. By the time
I had grown and been taught how to use a gun the 'crake wasn't
heard nearly so often. We no longer had men who could mow

and might be left to cut hay in one field while some other work was undertaken elsewhere. In the neighbouring fields, beyond our marches, the rolling acres of hay and corn were harvested by the use of two and sometimes three machines one behind the other, with as many as nine horses plodding along the sward.

All at once the call of the corncrake became a novel sound. My grandmother, had she lived, wouldn't have said her nerves were troubled by the incessant crying of the 'crakes. Far out, in the remote back country where the narrow, stony roads were tinged with the green of fine grass, the corncrake was still to be heard and the solitary workers in their quiet, tucked-away paddocks hardly knew that it was a bird that was becoming rare and dying out fast. Indeed, some old countrymen said that the corncrake had simply gone silent; it was a secret bird; it had always been of that habit. This, of course, was a fairy story.

I remember one day walking the bog field and putting up a brown bird which I shot almost by instinctive reaction. It was a corncrake. In the old days people had considered them an excellent table bird. I was dismayed to find that I had killed one. I didn't know what to do. To hide my guilt I tucked the bird into the pocket of my jacket. I went on walking the bog and shot a hare, which I took home for someone to make into soup. I hung my jacket behind the door and forgot it and in due course the dead bird advertised its presence and my crime was discovered.

'This is a corncrake,' said the old man sadly. 'You've killed a corncrake. Now what have I told you about shooting a bird you couldn't name?'

I had confessed that I had shot without thought, without identifying the bird. Would I have shot a barn owl? I wouldn't have been so foolish. I knew a barn owl. I knew every bird that took wing before me, if I gave myself time to think, to collect my wits. If I was to go on shooting I would have to learn to

7

be cautious! There was no excuse for wanton shooting and that included the destruction not only of birds like the corncrake, but an excessive number of any kind. If I brought a brace of pheasants from the bracken along the woodside I had shot enough for one day, perhaps even for a week, and I must never walk after the partridges until I destroyed a covey.

To be quite honest I never shot with any other outlook than the test of my skill, the provision of birds for the table, a thought that what I left undisturbed would be there to fly again and breed; and I had enough to train my eye in the shape of the crow, the magpie, the stoat, although for some reason the old man had a soft spot for stoats, which he said came closer to the farm when the first ricks were threshed out. Partridges always came under a more kindly regard than any other bird of the field, perhaps because they have no arrogance, because they are brave little birds and belong to the furrow the way a domestic fowl belongs to the farmyard.

Not everywhere were they preserved so well in or out of the breeding season. They were netted – and trapped – by the poachers of the locality. When the estate was shot, large numbers were bagged on the root fields, although the heavy shooting may have balanced the preservation methods used by the keepers. The Euston system had great advantages so far as a large area of both arable and rough was concerned. The partridges that might have been left exposed to predators were harvested in the closer confines of the breeding pens. When at length they were fledged they had extensive root fields near the home farm in which to find shelter. Keepers laid sheltering branches and bushes for the little birds where shelter was scarce or lacking altogether, and feeding kept a good number of birds from straying to the less well-protected fringes. It was fortunate that this was done because the wild stocks fluctuated, even in those days. Partridges have always been prone to particular ailments. Time and circumstances were against them. As the equipment of harvesting improved and social changes took place, the partridge would face new hazards and, although they were by no means a rare bird, and one could put up large coveys in almost every sizeable field, we were to see a decline.

If the history of the fluctuations in the numbers of ground birds and ground-nesting birds could be traced to anything in particular, it would be possible to mark the dates of change, but the fluctuations had subtle causes – war, changes in the economy of the big estate, the revolution in machinery, in farming methods and cropping. To begin with a relatively simple line, the partridge was affected by the mechanisation of hay-making. It was subsequently robbed of cover by silage making, by the catch-cropping of rich aftergrowth in which young birds might shelter, by the grubbing out of hedges and the enlargement of cultivated fields, by the ploughing of headlands closer to the bank, the reclamation of scrub, the grubbing of bracken and gorse and the use of selective weed-killers and sprays.

Had the old keepers remained at their posts, had they not faded away and died without heirs, had it not been profitable to sell timber or anything else that graced estates but could be turned to cash, the partridge would not have been under pressure serious enough to make it local and rare. Five or six years of war, in fact, almost reduced it to its natural status, a bird that could only survive as the 'crake had survived into my generation, on the fringe and far out on the wild hill where it took its chance without protection, decimated by the multitude of predators that a war had allowed to multiply.

Are there as many partridges as there once were? The well-keepered estates in the southern parts of the country show good figures. There are places particularly suited to the partridge's breeding and survival, despite all the things that might detract on the side of agricultural techniques, but one doesn't need to have made a great study of the pattern of country life and rural occupations to know that keepers are fewer and far between. Men who know how to look after game are as rare as some of our rare birds. Intensive rearing is costly and almost a thing of the past, except in a few places. Few men want to take a situation that ties them to the field for almost twenty-four hours of the day in the breeding season, and boys to help in the task are not to be found. We must sigh and say that nature has restored the balance; and the situation is one that might only be preserved by moderation and restraint.

This applies in every sphere of sport where the pressure has built up in a more affluent society. There are more people who would like to shoot and fish than ever before, but our resources are small. If every tyro filled his bag the outlook for the following season would be bleak. The wild partridge, as opposed to the bird that is sheltered and cared for within the confines of a few big estates of keepered syndicates, is, after all, a native British bird. It has been holding its own in the wilderness for a long, long time. It was never really plentiful, but it had its seasons and waves of increase and decline as most other native wild creatures have had.

At times one hears it suggested that the little brown bird should be protected completely, the hope being that it might become numerous and common everywhere, but it seems pretty plain that the partridge has not merely to be protected in order to multiply. It needs to be fostered, fed, gathered in, cultivated – and who would undertake this fantastic task? Shooting the peregrine is one way to ensure that bird's extinction, but to prohibit its destruction is not to guarantee its increase, for it lives on a territory and is predatory, requiring a certain fertile acreage to provide it with its prey. The partridge eats insects, grass, seed and grain.

It does no great harm, but it remains an item of diet for predatory creatures and it is part of the balance. To give it protection all the year round, without destroying large numbers of stoats, weasels, rats and crows, would most likely result in better-fed vermin. No man who shoots even a small acreage of ground fails to realise that he competes with a host of other killers and even when the vermin are checked there are greater hazards in the shape of diseases.

There were more partridges in my youth, the old men still say. This is true. The acreage of farmland has diminished, the techniques of harvesting have improved and the keepers have gone, but the partridge will hold its own with the wild pheasant or any other bird that attracts predators because it is well adapted to the rough hill as well as to the meadow and the plough, and it will not be driven away because it couldn't adapt itself to anywhere but the long grass. Its extinction is unlikely to be threatened and shooting interests will take a great deal of credit for the level of numbers from year to year, in spite of the interpretation some people chose to give the figures after great partridge drives in places such as East Anglia.

I have never shot driven partridges. It was never my lot to shoot in places where partridges could be driven. I have walked the root field and put up partridges from the long tunnels of kale or the forest of rape. They are not always the hardest of birds to hit, but they are capable of turning and speeding away low over the ground, knowing, perhaps, what every trout fisherman should know, that background is the most important thing in concealment. Coveys have a habit of erupting all at once from a small patch of ground and putting the shooter's nerves and co-ordination to the test. The man who isn't able to control himself to pick his bird and give it time finds the startled partridge a difficult target, whether there is clear sky and plenty of room round it or not.

Like the snipe or the woodcock, the partridge sits tight to choose its moment. It not only hears the disturbance of the leaves of the root field, it feels the vibration of the ground. It moves forward as unobtrusively as the corncrake when it feels that it has a chance of eluding the approaching guns. It sits tight when it knows that pursuit is relentless and danger closer than the bank or the hedge.

They are handsome little birds and tasty things to encounter under the protection of a silver cover, if one enjoys the flavour of game. They are rich and luscious and fit to make a supper for a king and I have fed on more than I now have hairs on my head. Matching my skill against the partridge has lost much of its attraction because I have come to see them more and more as small fowl, like diminutive chickens of the field, looking round from the top of a mound, gathering at nightfall to form some sort of mutual defence out in the grass of the pasture.

If I must confess it, I have become a sentimentalist about the partridge. Perhaps the reason for this goes back to the days when I was a boy and the partridges were plentiful on the home paddocks. More often than not a venturesome hen would bring her growing covey right down to the territory of the free-range hens and encourage them to pick seeds and insects where the pullets were feeding or take shelter where the hens were dust-bathing. There was something so disarming about this behaviour that even when it happened after the harvest was in, and guns were beginning to visit the rootfields, no one would dream of shooting the birds that came close to the door. Oddly enough no one ever questioned this fact. It was understood and if half the partridges of the fields came close to home they would have been immune.

Is the hill partridge a different sort of bird? Some people say that it is, just as there are some people who would describe the lake trout as a separate species or sub-species of the river trout. I am not sure about this. When I had nothing but my modest experience to guide me I used to think that there were two kinds of hare apart from the variable or mountain hare. The bog hares seemed bigger and their colouring was a shade darker I found. This was no doubt a local variation. Hares that frequented the open arable fields and ran the higher hills never seemed to be so big or heavy as the hares I shot in the lower meadows. Hill partridges are not only wilder, but here in Wales I often found a darker, more brown partridge, the partridge of the arable fields tending to be greyer. This, too, must be a matter of diet and adaption to background.

If the egg of a plover that lays on a pasture is often shades darker and more green than that of the same species laying on the brown furrow, it is reasonable to suggest that generations of wild partridges confined to hill and scrubland show a variation in plumage. They may not be classified as a sub-species, but it hardly matters. A hill partridge is a hill partridge, feeding slightly less, perhaps, on one sort of food than another and even acquiring a particular flavour as a result. There is nothing wilder than a hill partridge covey that rises and sweeps away on the wind, contouring the ground, gliding for brief periods as they skim a drystone wall or top a thorn hedge. The way these wild birds alight always seems to indicate a greater alertness than is shown by the pasture breed. They drop, stand a moment or two and look about, run forward and take cover before they move on. They are hardly ever to be put up where they alight and they survive as a result of the pattern of their life, stalked by vermin from the wall and the hedge, waited upon by crow and hawk and hounded by people who mark their locality and favourite places for sun-bathing and dust-bathing at the noon hour.

Walking up a hill covey requires a certain fieldcraft, for, like the grouse on the moor, the hill partridge, when it takes its ease on the rough ground, has already studied the lie of the land and although it may be stalked upwind it will turn as soon as it gets the chance and present that difficult curving, dropping target so easily missed. The man who gets his brace will often admit to having had luck. The man who misses will hesitate before he plods on to try to come up with the birds again. Not every hillside supports a covey and often the die is cast when the first opportunity is missed. Let those who have experienced every difficult shot there is say what they like about driven partridges induced to fly high and turn with the wind in their favour, the wild hill partridge has nothing to be ashamed of in the way it can keep close to its background and mislead all but the keenest eye!

GUN GLAMOUR

◇◇◇◇◇◇◇◇◇◇◇◇◇◇◇◇◇◇◇◇◇◇◇◇◇

LONG before I had acquired any ability with a gun I became fascinated by the gunmaker's art and admired the engraving on the finer guns I saw. Hammerless guns were handsomely engraved and stream-lined until they had the grace of swans, a sort of handleability that made me want to touch them, but the older hammer guns were often even more graceful in appearance, and the Damascus barrel with that spiral of figuring had a special beauty belonging to another generation. All sorts of guns came and went when I was a child. All sorts of people came to shoot and brought their weapons with them. On some of these guns the hammers stood like pug dogs and on others they had the nobility of the arched neck of a blood horse. The stocks of most guns are made of walnut, but not all of them, and the grain and finish of a stock was as great a delight to me as the chasing on the screws of the metal parts and the perfect in-setting of locks in the wood of the stock itself.

All this I saw in guns when I was five or six years old – their proportions, their balance, their shape, their ornamentation, meant something to me and even the ancient converted rifle that lay in an outhouse had a certain hand-worn polish about it, a glamour which I found in the poacher's folding gun with the octagonal barrel, the old muzzle-loader, the shaky underlever that one of the men took with him to the plough on the pretext of shooting crows, but in fact to knock over an unwary cock pheasant out of season.

I have owned not a few guns in my life and my present gun is what is known as a semi-automatic, but still hanging in the house is the first gun I ever owned, an old hammer-gun with a paper-thin Damascus barrel. I shot my first rabbit with that gun. Both my father and grandfather had shot with it. It was almost an antique when it was given to me, although it was sound enough for the old black-powder cartridges. There was a silver-disc inset in the dark wood of the stock, but the initials of the original owner had worn off. My son has killed many a pigeon and not a few pheasants with it, so that four generations of us have walked the fields with it and it has become a family heirloom.

In the pedantically written manuals of shooting one often comes across the recommendation that a boy's first gun should be a ·410, the smaller and lighter gun being easier to handle and giving less recoil to the shoulder. I sometimes wonder if the experts were not too pampered in their youth, or might it have been that they were somewhat puny and timid? I used a twelve-bore when I was ten years of age. It didn't, as far as I can remember, rock me or knock me off my feet. Only very rarely have I ever been conscious of a gun's impact on my shoulder and not by any means can I claim that every gun I fired was a first-class example of the gunmaker's art.

I have fired all kinds of cartridges, all kinds of loads from all kinds of fowling pieces, and I am inclined to think that the fault in nine cases out of ten lies in the beginner not holding the gun naturally and as firmly as might be needed to make any implement do what it is required to do. The twelve-bore is a heavier gun than a fourteen, of course, but a youngster who can't manage to carry a light twelve should stay at home and take nourishment. There are intermediate stages that the gunroom expert may advocate – the use of a twenty- or a sixteen-bore. The little gun seems to be a needless restriction and the sixteen has always seemed to me to be a bit of a fad. It kills a hare or a goose, but it is almost like pitching sheaves with a short-handled fork, toasting muffins and burning one's knuckles.

The gun I was given was the one I was to use for my whole apprenticeship. It was neat and not too heavy, a fair example of the gunmaker's art and it would do until time had taught me what I wanted. I couldn't have a gun tailored to fit me and,

like many another tyro, I had to fit myself to the gun – which isn't the tragedy that some people might think. No youngster remains physically the same. His shoulders broaden, the bones of his body lengthen and he grows to manhood as a sapling grows to be a tree. The gun that fitted him at eighteen doesn't exactly suit his build when he is in his physical prime and as the man ages, thickens, stiffens, the gun needs to be modified as a well-worn old tweed suit would have to be let out and altered. A gun that fits certainly reduces the chances of a poor performance, but even so it doesn't fit quite so well when a man wears different clothing, changes his light shooting coat for a thicker one to go fowling on the marsh and so on.

Although in time I came to appreciate the doctoring of a gun to make it come up to the shoulder better, to change its balance and remedy one's own physical defects, I was content with the gun they gave me. It was a delight to my eye and it was hardly ever out of my hands. When I wasn't carrying it in the field I was wiping it over with a soft cloth, inspecting the barrels for fouling, looking for the smallest specks of dirt, the slightest suspicion of a spot of rust. I ruefully admit that in the first few months it was mine it must have suffered more wear through being stripped and reassembled than it would have done in a decade of ordinary use in the field. It belonged in my hands, it nestled in the crook of my arm. When there was no one to supervise me I followed flights of far-off duck, swung to flocks of starlings, took quick snap shots at flies, startled rabbits, galloping hares. I expended ten thousand imaginary cartridges with ten thousand combinations of rights and lefts, but I didn't let the hammers fall on empty chambers because that, I had been told, would do the nipples no good, would put extra wear on the springs of the hammers, the locks and the firing pins. I knew every screw and stud of the gun's mechanism. My father was an engineer of some ability. My grandfather had invented agricultural implements, and if I had no gift of the same sort yet I understood a mechanism.

Day after day, year after year, I shot with this gun. I worried about it when I was away and when I returned for the holidays I suffered from anxiety in case someone had taken it to scare crows, laid it beside a drystone wall and damaged the barrels, or committed some other folly that might have ruined its efficiency. I could tell if anyone had tampered with it because I always put it away in perfect order. I knew every mark on every part of that gun. It was a priceless thing in my estimation. It is no use pretending that this passion arose from the discovery that I was a natural shot. I was not. There aren't many people who are so gifted. It is an instinct that goes with perfect co-ordination of hand and eye, an instinct obviating a need for anyone to put lead into diagram or illustrate swing. One can acquire skill, but a gift is prenatal.

I remember my first running shot. It wasn't an easy shot. I had been taken out that summer's evening to stalk and shoot a few of the hundreds of rabbits that swarmed on every bank and along every woodside in my part of the world in those days. Entering a large meadow I put up a rabbit from a small gorse bush and the rabbit ran along a sheep track, going downhill and curving to the right. It set its ears back and went for all it was worth. My instructor said: 'Well, what are you waiting for?' I did my best to swing through along the line of the sheep track, but it was all too quick for deliberation. I pulled and the rabbit tumbled head over heels and lay still. I suppose I poked at it. Perhaps it was a case of an accidental interception. I would miss often enough to discover that there were right and wrong ways of taking such shots – and cartridges were nearly tuppence each!

Soon after this I tried to shoot a flying pigeon. It was one of those shots without background, without perspective in the deep blue of the sky. There was no reason in the world, it seemed to me, why the bird should have continued to fly, but it did; it rose to the height it wanted, flattened out, turned a wing and went round in a half-mile circle. It never wavered although I watched it, until at length it went out of sight. How high had it been? I judged the height of a pine tree, but I knew nothing of elementary trigonometry. Perhaps it had been sixty yards off when I fired? The old hammergun was hardly a far-reaching piece. It was bored cylinder and quarter choke and I had to learn to judge distance with accuracy.

It has always seemed to me that some people with remarkably good long sight have a sort of fixed-focus vision when there is no background. They must find the range. Until they do they either mutilate their birds or tickle them with a pellet or two, which is worse. All at once this judgment seemed to come to me. I suppose I was about sixteen when I knew I could shoot, the gun was part of my body, an extension of my arm and eye. Everything I had been told about swing, lead, balance, foot-movement seemed to come naturally or didn't matter. I hadn't discovered a gift, but I had acquired confidence. People began to say that I could shoot. They said it rather too often and I think, on reflection, that, if the gun almost fitted, my hat hardly ever did, but now and again I had the benefit of shooting with a man who was a natural, old McWilliam, the finest shot I have ever known.

Old McWilliam was a retired farmer. He spent a good deal of his time calling on his former colleagues and enjoying a day's shooting. His gift was extraordinary and he was quite unaware that it was a gift. He was puzzled to think that other people couldn't do what he could do and he had absolutely no ability to teach. His advice was brief: give the bird time, give it distance, shoot smoothly and quickly. It sounded very easy. He corrected my mistakes quietly, neatly, in the only way he knew, by bringing down the things I missed!

There is one great advantage in doing anything in the company of an expert, and that is that the example banishes all standards save perfection or as near perfection as the expert can demonstrate. I began to judge myself by old McWilliam. I couldn't hope to achieve the things he did so effortlessly, but at least I knew that I wasn't a good shot. I had a long, long way to go. The snipe rose from the mud at the gate or on the bog and I saw how old McWilliam dealt with them. He certainly shot without apparent hurry. He shot deliberately yet without seeming to deliberate. He wasn't so much a calm man as a man who was never flustered. He was impatient, hot-tempered and his blood pressure went up alarmingly when I blundered, but he was never anything else but a cool shot. He never blamed his gun, the cartridges or the light, the wind, the dog or anything else, although he blamed me for missing things he seemed convinced I had tried to miss.

We got on famously when I shot well. I always tried to avoid meeting him at the gate or the end of the rough if I had made a mess of things. Sometimes we changed over guns. The old man seemed to think that anything that was capable of firing a cartridge was capable of hitting a bird. It wasn't the gun, it was the man. This isn't true, of course. The better a gun comes to the shoulder the better a man's average will be. If guns were no more than drain pipes, the great gunsmiths would have had no higher reputation than the duffers – and the great shots wouldn't have recorded such great bags. One grows up with a gun, but it isn't really the answer any more than growing up with the same pair of boots is the answer to the problem of walking well. Old McWilliam's gun had been selected (if it hadn't actually been built for him) after years of gun-handling. He had probably discarded ten or a dozen good guns until he found one that suited him, but he had forgotten that.

Sooner or later, whether the glamour of fine gunsmithing wears off or not, whether one has an eye for beauty or not, most enthusiasts begin to toy with the idea that eventually leads to the shooting school, and, if they can afford it, having a gun fitted to their physical characteristics. I began to suspect, as I filled out and grew longer in the arm, that the handsome old hammergun wasn't the answer to my problem. I could shoot fairly well with it, but I no longer shot with confidence. I bought a new gun, a hammerless gun, sound and solid, by one of the famous gunsmiths. I didn't shoot particularly well with it, but I managed a very difficult shot with it on my first outing and I was convinced that it would make me the shot I hoped to be!

Quite apart from the fetish of guns and their varying features — cast-on, cast-off, high-comb, low-comb, balance, length, weight, most gun fanatics know the danger of developing fads (a friend of mine who is a very fine clay-pigeon shot varies his tipple from season to season or meeting to meeting, relaxing himself one day with a small glass of cider, the next with a tot of rum and the next with some sherry or madeira) and I was about to embark on the journey through the maze. My hammerless was bored too tight. I must have one barrel recessed. I had that done. It didn't seem to make much difference, but then the stock was too short. I needed an extension piece inserted between the butt-plate and the wood of the stock. This was done. I went on missing to the same degree as before and turned to an old single-barrelled gun that was as heavily choked as the left barrel of the double had been and, moreover, had an almost straight stock. The stock of this gun proved too short and I lengthened it more than I needed to have done. The comb was too low. I was bringing my head down. I built up the comb. A good gunsmith or shooting instructor could have eliminated the multiplicity of errors with which I confused the point until I came back to the

beginning, removed the extension to the butt and the build-up on the comb – and put the gun from me!

A rather fine hammerless ejector followed. It was a fowling piece and a little heavy. It was heavily choked, too, and although I admired it I couldn't make much of a showing with it when I carried it in the field. In the end I traded it away for fishing tackle and talked about having lost what little skill I had had.

By misfortune the stock of the old Damascus-barrelled gun was shattered and for sentimental reasons I had a new one fitted, although the gun was unfit for proofing. I toyed with the idea of using the one ounce loads that would have made the ancient gun usable, but returned, instead, to the single and to the straight left-arm way of shooting. In theory, it seemed to me that a good straight left arm was the same thing as pointing one's finger, and with the right swing a man should be able to shoot much better if he could persuade himself to hold the gun in that manner. Unfortunately, I had never been able to do this. I had grown up with the weakness and to eliminate it I made a new foreend for the single and notched it in such a fashion that I was compelled to hold the gun as far up the barrel as the foreend reached. I didn't shoot well at first, but after a season I began to find that it came naturally to me to keep a straight left arm and all at once I found my average improving. At pigeons I did much better than I had ever done. I shot quickly and neatly, but more important still, I shot with complete confidence.

The limitations of every man are with him from the day he is born until the day he dies, but within limits there are results governed by over-confidence or lack of confidence. Faith is something one cultivates within – or destroys – with consequent effect upon one's performance at any sport. I could shoot reasonably well when I was eighteen. I shot badly when I understood how far removed I was from the sphere of the expert. I improved immensely when I restored my confidence and stopped comparing my ability with that of men I could never hope to equal. No matter what the expert says, there is a great deal in believing in the fly at the end of one's cast or the cartridges in the gun – the gun itself.

Fads and fetishes are not to be laughed at if they produce the result, and the man who takes his stand to shoot clay pigeons feeling that the gun can do it and that cider is exactly the thing to take the edge off his nerves is as well off as his neighbour who takes only a biscuit for lunch convinced that he is keener and sharper when his stomach is being gnawed at.

I came, in the end, to a gun that hasn't the glamour of the finer examples of the gunsmith's art – a semi-automatic with a ventilated rib, some characterless engraving and sling swivels. I changed because I found I could shoot well with this type of gun and it is eminently suited for pigeons and wildfowling. Five shots give no particular advantage either to the man who can shoot well or to the indifferent shot, for very rarely will the crack shot be certain of three kills and only once in a lifetime of four or five, while the indifferent shot can as easily pump three shots into the clear air as he can one or two when his swing is wrong. It helps, however, when one stands a long time on a cold winter's day waiting for pigeons to flight to know that the gun is loaded with five cartridges and can be reloaded with little trouble when a lull comes. The heavier gun is an aid to steadiness and in my experience the recoil is undetectable. No one proposing to walk miles over a large rough shoot can afford to discount the weight of a gun and the automatic is a little heavier than the average game gun, but I am fortunate in not being troubled in this way, contenting myself with flying birds.

A good automatic takes a lot of beating, I think, but it is all entirely a matter of personal taste. No one should shoot with a gun because it is handsome or has a beautiful mechanism, but because he believes in it and this applies to any kind of gun, underlever, hammerless, pump, semi-automatic, single, double, over and under or gas gun. They say that the standard double is a balanced gun and can't be improved upon. They say that a single teaches a shot to swing and be accurate because he has no chance of a second barrel. They say that the automatic is a sweet weapon and free from recoil and that the pump eliminates the danger of sending one useless shot after another. There are still a few people about who swear by black powder for smoothness and sweet shooting. They say everything, in fact, that can be said about every sort of gun in fashion, and all of it is true – if one has faith, if one believes, and all other things are equal. One's tongue can only be in one cheek at a time, but the answer is to be found outside in the field when the goose stops in mid-air and comes down like a bomber, when the snipe crumples, the pheasant's flight becomes an acute arc as he crashes on to the meadow, or the speeding hare trips and goes head-over-heels to lie in a heap. Look down at the gun then and admire its engraving, its efficient mechanism, its slender stock, or consider what it lacks that would give it glamour, but none of it could make it do more than stop the bird!

SECRETS OF SNIPE

FADING light and a haze of fine rain, a flooded corner of an old pasture with rich loam beneath the mat of the turf are things synonymous with snipe in my recollections of them. One can walk a snipe bog and put the roosting snipe up at different times of the short winter day or catch them early when they are busy in the muddy places where the hooves of sheep or store cattle have churned the almost bare earth, but the best place to see snipe is on their regular feeding ground at certain times of the year. They come in twos or threes, quickly, unexpectedly, showing against the grey sky for a minute or two, as exciting to glimpse as the rise of a feeding trout after a long period of inactivity. The watcher becomes part of the motionless background and the snipe come in. There is a magic to it, just as there is magic in the twilight flight of the heron, the owl, the nightjar and waterbirds of all kinds.

The snipe is nocturnal, like many other birds that search marshy ground for delicacies. It is not so much elusive as secret in its habits. One bird nearest to the gate or the ditch decides that the moment has come to take to the air and away it goes, arcing into the mist, and it seems at times that this first bird to spring from the mud is attached by an invisible thread to another, and a second springs up, bringing up another almost at once – one on a shorter thread, perhaps, twisting in another direction. The thing is triggered off and the birds rise here, there and everywhere, without regularity, without pattern, but ultimately heading in the same general direction and always, always leaving that very last straggler to take flight with startling suddenness and small chance of being shot or intercepted.

What pattern can one make of the snipe, resident and local migrant, in its day-to-day movements? It is hard to make a map of the snipe's places because, as with the fish in the river or lake, they are affected by changes in temperature, by the rising of the water in the drains and ditches, by the congealing of the mud, the hardening of certain tracts of ground, the cold breath of the wind from the east, a change in barometric pressure. These things influence the reproduction of insects, the changes in larval life in the mud, the movement of snails, worms.

It necessarily follows that although snipe flight to a pasture on the fringe of more boggy ground, they change their habit immediately the ground begins to freeze. The worms are safe. Their movements are puzzling because their built-in predictors make it unnecessary for them to visit their former feeding place to discover the change. As the change comes, some instinct prompts them to seek a feeding place that is more sheltered, just as the woodcock moves out of exposed copses to ground where the thick carpet of dead leaves provides some insulation from the paralysing effect of hard frost. The delights of searching for snipe are enhanced by the element of surprise because the snipe feeds in a certain place and spends a little longer finding its food when conditions are hard. Not every place where snipe roost or sleep the middle of the day away is easily walked in winter. Their roosting bogs are as well chosen as the shelter sought by water-birds and when they are disturbed the odds are in their favour.

The snipe shot is generally one who has the opportunity of visiting the resident haunt of snipe as often as he wants. It isn't hard to shoot a snipe, but it takes a certain degree of skill to make a bag and rather special co-ordination to achieve right and lefts regularly! The secret of the snipe shot's performance is the elementary secret of accumulated experience. Marking a snipe on the bog or in waterlogged pasture is far beyond the average man's ability. He may have the thing done for him sometimes, but most of the time, and even when a dog has somehow given him sign, there remains the unexpected rising of the bird, its slashing flight, first into the air and then perhaps towards the horizon in an arc.

How to shoot is a matter for the man with the gun. He may watch the expert, but the business is more split-second than his eye may comprehend, and the way to make a bag of snipe is as arduous for the ungifted as the way of filling a creel with good trout. The shot who has a snipe bog under his jurisdiction and more than one feeding ground within his boundary is blessed indeed. His apprenticeship is at least possible. When his friends describe him as a snipe shot he has something more than average skill; he is a member of a very select company when he is able to go out and bring back enough snipe to grace a respectable roasting pan.

Because the snipe season begins on the Glorious Twelfth and continues right through until the end of January, the snipe shooter, or the rough shooter who is glad to take things as they come, may find himself recording his bag in the game book and listing three sorts of snipe – the little jack snipe, the full snipe and the double snipe, the latter two sometimes being described as the common snipe and the great snipe. The identification of fowl is one of the things every ardent shooting man strives to be able to do at an early age. It isn't hard to tell the little jack snipe from the full snipe. Its habit is so distinctive. It rises and flies something like a bat that flickers from one clump of trees to the next. It pitches from place to place as though reluctant to take a long flight. It is much easier to bring down because it hasn't the real jinking ability of the full snipe, but if it is simply recorded in the game book as a snipe it tends to enhance the reputation of the party a little beyond its due.

The great snipe might be more easily mistaken for a woodcock than a common snipe if one had next to no knowledge of these birds. It doesn't have the flushing, aerobatic ability of the full snipe. It shows a broad tail and it is encountered mainly in September, being a passage migrant. It is in fact sometimes called a woodcock snipe. The jack snipe is a pathetic thing to put on a dish more than once. It belongs, I think, to the bad old days when larks and turtle doves were shot and all was grist to the mill until there were no birds to be found on the common land, the bustard eliminated and quail brought to the verge of extinction. Shooting jack snipe is like hounding golden plover when they first come in. The common snipe, our own native bird that has its numbers increased by large numbers of wintering snipe, is by far the finest bird of the snipe family and in my opinion puts the woodcock – the bottle bird, if one can achieve a right and left – completely to shame for speed and unpredictability, and it is never sluggish, like the cock of the wood.

I used to walk a snipe bog where sometimes snipe were as thick on the ground as feeding starlings. It was an electrifying experience to visit the bog on certain days. Snipe were everywhere, along the fringes of great pools of clear water in which several feet of sphagnum were submerged, among the rushes and along the narrow tracks on hard ground where the sheep had negotiated their way from one island of fine grass to the next. The rising of snipe would begin like the lifting of leaves in the wind. Before one had walked ten yards on a bright morning the snipe would be off to some secondary roosting ground, for they lived on the bog by day and took themselves off at night.

It was never profitable to walk the bog before noon. The morning sun seemed to keep the snipe alert and ready to go. Perhaps they still bored for worms here and there. Perhaps they simply settled to contemplate the morning sky and didn't really roost until afternoon, but in the afternoon it was different. They rose then with less spontaneity, and fell back like a regiment withdrawing in good order, so that if one had the eye and the ability to shoot with certain deliberation it was possible to make a bag.

To be truthful I found for a long time that my self-confidence wasn't up to snipe shooting. I used to talk about my gun being too tightly bored, the pattern being too dense. Number seven shot was all very well, but I needed something better. The simple answer was that I lacked practice. A man has to expend a few cartridges to make good figures at clays, at pigeons or any other sort of bird, and I hadn't the knack of snipe shooting. I was put off by the zig-zag flight and the advice I was given from time to time. I could never remember the advice when it came to the point. I was full of it until the snipe were touched off and the moment the first one was suddenly plastered against the sky

everything went out of my head. I shot and generally missed. If I had two barrels I missed twice. I hesitated the next time. I missed for different reasons. The snipe left the bog or all but one or two left and then, when I came to the boundary, the stragglers would suddenly rise and I would miss again. It was like trying to shoot gnats and I couldn't afford to go on making a hash of things.

I can't say when my luck changed or when I acquired the way of taking snipe as they came. It wasn't on the bog where I could shoot when I pleased, and as often as I liked. By the time I had found the secret the bog was no longer accessible to me and never again was I to see the snipe rise in such numbers. The snipe bog of my youth is a nostalgic memory. I shall never see its like again.

Although the snipe is a bird of the bog and the moor, and roosts in this sort of place, it takes its meals in very different grounds. It loves sewage farms and marshy, muddy hollows of all kinds. It flights at nightfall, but it isn't a bird to be flighted as duck or other birds might be. It dallies in the early day before it returns to roost and it is to be put up by the casual shooter making his round of the rough ground.

Five snipe on a dish are not enough to feed three people, but they take some shooting. They are a gourmet's dish, something for the epicure who knows they must be cooked without being drawn. They are a supreme test of the shooter's skill and should be carried to the kitchen with a certain pride. They are best eaten by those who know what the habits of snipe are, just as the best whisky should be offered only to those who know what good whisky is. Let Mrs Beeton advise on their treatment, but be cautious about recipes requiring a dozen birds, unless you have some experts among your companions, and a bog beloved of snipe coming west for the winter as they regularly do.

When you have studied the snipe – and it is the duty of every man who shoots to study and show some concern for the welfare of his quarry – you will find that it has a delightful way of dropping down to the bog at times, half closing its wings and pitching down, and that it will sit on a post or take a short upward flight and drum its wings as it moves through the air. It nests on the bog and lays an egg a little bigger than the egg of the sandpiper. Its chick is as elusive as the chick of any moorbird and a perfect blend with its surroundings. There are times when the adult snipe makes a cry when it is on the ground, although those who disturb snipe generally only hear the scraping call that it gives in alarm as it speeds off. It is this cry that brings the next bird, close at hand, into the air and sets the wisp into flight.

In the breeding season things are ordered differently and the snipe, as well as the snipe's nest, is hard to find among the bog cotton and the grasses, the heather and ling, as hard to come upon as the nest of the nightjar; much harder to trace than that of the grouse or the curlew, in my opinion.

Some of the best snipe shooting to be had anywhere is found in Ireland, because Ireland's winter climate is more suitable to the snipe's ways, particularly if a cold wind from the east is followed by snow. Large numbers of snipe that would feed on the marshes and pastures of England, Wales and Scotland wind up on the other side of the Irish Sea and return only when conditions have mellowed in March. Many of the wintering snipe move east and north on their return and it would be hard to say just what sort of breeding population we have, but judging from the numbers one encounters in the off-season the snipe is reasonably secure and plentiful. It is in no great danger of being decimated by shooting for the simple reason that it is a more than somewhat difficult bird to intercept. No one who has tried his hand at snipe shooting would wish it to be otherwise. If the snipe could be brought down by throwing one's hat at it no one would want to shoot it.

Who taught it to be so elusive in flight, to jink and twist and arc and somehow look like rough stitching in the sky? I fancy man did when he began to throw his club at it, and then his spear, his arrow, his blunderbus's load, and finally his ounce or so of chilled number seven shot. All this took several thousand generations and the snipe is still one up, despite all the theory of lead and swing, the smoothness of the perfect mechanism, smokeless powder and the rest. No sportsman would enjoy it otherwise and one thing is certain – there will never be a day in this country at any rate when five or six guns record four hundred snipe apiece at a day's shooting. The snipe will always be to me the same as the wild trout I sometimes take on the dry fly – something with everything in its favour, a master of tactics in its own element.

THE WAYS OF WOODCOCK

LEST my admiration for the snipe be taken as contempt for the woodcock, and an implication that I consider myself a master woodcock shot, I must hurry to say that I have never been in a position to write to Humberts with the name of a witness to testify to my right and left; but in common with not a few who shoot the rough and walk the wood, I have achieved a right and left at woodcock more than once – without a witness – and I fancy before the bottle was on offer! The woodcock may be considered to zig-zag with more deliberation than the snipe, but if there is any advantage in it, or disadvantage, it is too split-second to make much difference to the shooter. Where the woodcock loses his gilt is when he rises from the bracken or undergrowth on a damp day, when the ground is soft and the air is still.

I can't say that I have ever noticed that the snipe has an off-day. Its habit is to frequent rather more open terrain. It may be that the moisture that affects the fibres of the quills and pinion feathers of the woodcock doesn't affect the feathers of the snipe, or that the haunts of snipe are more airy and less inclined to hold the heavy moisture that keeps the woodcock down. The moor and the marsh are giving off moisture nearly all the time, and it rises freely, while in the heart of the wood dampness positively hangs in the air at times. Whatever the reason, the woodcock has a day when he rises and flaps away like an old hen. His going is almost owl-like and if he turns round a tree one can see that he hasn't any intention of beating high and going far. He almost always drops down again a hundred yards on.

On the cold frosty morning how different he is! No longer magnified by the mist, he is a slim, fast bird, quick to rise over the hazels, off with the speed of a hawk hedge-hopping in pursuit of a frightened finch. Woodcock may doze by day, but when the ground is hard they take the ground signal as accurately as any bird that walks the floor of the wood. Their senses are as acute as the old cock pheasant that crows at the far-off thunder or the quarry blasting, and the smallest vibration is imparted to them as the man with the dog comes slowly through the wood. The woodcock's spring is as startling on a frosty day as the rise of any snipe. It can be breath-taking, heart-arresting, paralysing.

A double at woodcock isn't merely a matter of the ability to swing and change to swing on to another bird. All sorts of things make it unusual. For one thing the woodcock is not gregarious. It is found in ones and twos and sometimes threes or fours by pure chance. When one rises it is picking its moment and knows its escape route, but if there is a second bird in the same hollow it doesn't necessarily present itself at the same moment and if it does it may well have a different line of escape.

36

Woodcock spend much of the night boring under the dead leaves for food. Nowhere in a wood that may be hardening in winter are worms particularly plentiful, but they do live in the moist hollows and in places where a carpet of leaves holds off the frost, as other sundry items of the woodcock's diet do. When the feeding bird is working his way along he isn't accompanied by others as might be the case with a partridge covey. He is pottering in a detached way, sheltered by the darkness and stopping only to listen for the approach of his nocturnal enemies. This situation makes it a matter of luck that three or four birds are there to be flushed or shot within a reasonable radius. They must then rise with the right background and clear of obstruction for the skilled shot to make his double!

There are hundreds of rough shooters who mark the woodcock on their list and not a few are taken at drives, but few people indeed ever make a bag of them, and few who quickly repeat their right and left, although an old friend, who is dead now, once wrote to tell me that in his young days he once had four woodcock falling – two doubles which he brought off at a stand with the help of a loader. He didn't say how often he had performed feats of this sort, but he was, I believe, one of the best shots of his time and completely ambidextrous with shotgun and revolver.

Even on his off-day when he rises slowly (some people say that the slow bird is a larger variety and a newly arrived migrant) the woodcock has much in his favour, for he is a master of tactics, choosing the moment to go, keeping low in certain conditions and rising steeply to drop over a screen of branches on another occasion. When he is once more in the shelter of the dead bracken he may sit tight, making the shooter key his nerves, or rise almost unobtrusively to slip through behind a fat oak and seek the deeper cover beyond. He matches his wits with man and dog as every

wild thing does, and anyone who doesn't make a serious study of his quarry can never hope to show results.

The delight of working through a small wood or copse quite alone but for the dog is something that has to be experienced. It stimulates some atavistic instinct, so far as I am concerned, but it has little to do with the fact that I have a gun in my hand, for I am little dismayed to find that the woodcock has beaten me, that my swing has been defeated by intervening trees, by a turn as neatly made as any manoeuvre of the darting swift. Tactics are limited when one is shooting alone. No grand strategy has been arranged by wily keepers who know just how to stop the escape routes and bring up the flanks at various places. It is true that in the case of an organised drive birds are often shown to their best advantage so far as the day's bag may be concerned, but to me the walking up of a woodcock that sits in the undergrowth, a perfect blend with the dead brown leaves, has something of the personal element that I find in setting about the task of catching a particular fish in a particular pool.

The best woodcock ground I ever walked was part of a rough shoot, a place, my less enthusiastic friends said at the end of each day, especially designed for a man with one short leg. It consisted of a broad, steep slope covered with rather spindly birch, ash and hazel with occasional clumps of scrub oak. It was cut by four or five minor gullies and at least two deep ones. The two large gullies were boulder-strewn and formed the bed of a rushing torrent of water that was nowhere deep but frothed and foamed and roared after heavy rain. Along the sides of these gullies the ground was always boggy and the carpet of dead leaves was deep. Woodcock loved these places. There were openings in plenty for them to drop down at night, and they were there to be flushed in the morning if one had the heart to stand the arduous struggle through the shin-lacing brambles and fatiguing mats of wet bracken that blocked the way from one clearing to the next.

There was something special in a journey across that slope whether one ended with one or two birds or none at all. Stopping for a breather one looked right across at the haze hanging round distant mountain peaks and there, almost below one's elbow, would be the top of a fifty-foot-high tree, and away down below that, a muddy field, a thorn hedge dropping still lower to the stream that meandered down the valley, the white blocks of little farms with slate roofs and hens dotted about their yards. In each of the gullies cutting the slope there were shelves one attained with exertion that made the heart pound and on the brink of them one paused to steady shaking hands and regain control before the woodcock was disturbed and swept through the hazels to the next patch of cover.

Sometimes no woodcock was there, but a hare was startled from the bracken on the fringe and raced like a mad thing to hang for a moment, it seemed, on the very edge of an escarpment and then turn, kicking leaves and mouldering earth as it crossed instead of climbed, a far easier shot than the silent, slip-away flight of the woodcock, although one might poke at it or fail because of a restricted swing with one leg bent much more than the other and the slope crumbling under one's weight.

There were occasions and places where neither hare nor woodcock showed and only a wood pigeon presented itself, cannoning out of an ivied thorn and dropping fast into the valley down below, or crossing and going out of the field of view in a split second. The clattering and crowing protest of an isolated pheasant might be all one heard, but these were the incidental shocks or the things that contrived to sharpen wits and keep a man on his toes. It is hard to shoot a bird that drops down through trees of varying height, hard to take one zig-zagging and rising among holly, ash and birch, and few who like things well-ordered would chose to shoot such ground, but there are other delights in shooting than being spoon-fed! I find more pleasure in a single shot that tests my skill, and perhaps owes something to more than average luck, than having a bag of birds, especially when I have stood where they could not help but come and I could not help but bring them down because, for once, the wind hung them up there and my eye was in, and there was nothing to it.

When the woodcock rose along that slope I could not count on putting them up again until I reached the boundary. When the ground was hard and the trees stark and bare against that wintry light, I could rely on them rising quickly and giving me next to no chance. I was lucky sometimes and gathered a few quills for my hatband. Sometimes I knew that I was getting into bad habits, snapping off a shot that shouldn't have been fired, poking where the bird had been – and gone. On bad days I would put my failures down to my being out of condition, which was often true. Shooting should always be unhurried. The man who bustles his way through a wood disturbs more than he sees, teaches the dog bad habits, infects it with excitement, and has such a lack of steadiness that he might better raise his cap to the departing bird than salute it with a charge of shot.

It is strange that the woodcock has gathered a legend that no other bird can equal. It is credited with being able to splint its own leg and with carrying off its young resting between its thighs. I cannot dispute the woodcock's capacity to carry its young. I have never seen it happen, although I have seen the woodcock at the nest and found its eggs. Perhaps it does perform such a feat. Perhaps it has been disturbed when the chicks were sheltering under its body and a young bird has inadvertently been carried aloft and dropped some distance away, or maybe it does move the chicks when the ground has dried and food is hard to find, for sometimes this might involve ground hazards that could not otherwise be surmounted. The leg-splinting legend is an old one and perhaps arose from someone finding a bird with a rough splint on its leg or, more likely, a thick and deformed leg that had healed after a break, for the woodcock is badly equipped to use its beak for anything but boring for food and preening its feathers. I don't know any bird that could splint a leg!

Long ago the woodcock used to nest in a small spruce planting that bordered on the march wall of the farm on which I lived as a small boy. It was a bird that was known and seen in flight more often than it was seen on the ground. It had the fascination of the corncrake and snipe, and the nightjar, because its nest was so well-concealed. It was so hard to track down. Finding the nest of the night jar amounted to spying upon the flighting and feeding birds when they were active in the evening, catching moths for the young or feeding while the eggs were being laid or incubated. Finding the nest of the snipe had a certain amount of labour about it. One put up a stick or two and quartered a section of ground within bounds one hoped contained the nest. The woodcock was unaccommodating. It slipped in and out of the wood in the half-light. Where exactly it dropped down one couldn't determine. It became a matter of instinct, almost of clairvoyance, to detect the nest. The moor is rough and open. There are many banks and depressions that may shelter nesting birds, but it is only a matter of time and patience.

The woodcock has the whole uneven surface of the wood and all its trees in which to shelter. It may have chosen a site beneath some tall tree or on a mound above a patch of marshy ground. It is a blend with its surroundings and its eggs match the dead leaves that strew the wood in March. No one can search the whole floor of even a small wood and the eggs could be crushed before they are noticed. When they are found they provide one of the thrills of a lifetime. They are a secret uncovered. They have the mystical significance of unattended eggs of any wild creature. One sees that they are part of the vast pattern of survival and knows that, if they are detected, in a hundred other secret places they have remained undetected and unmolested. If here the sharp-eyed jay finds them or the hunting rat sucks the life out of them, elsewhere the same eggs are safely incubated and woodcock will still fly, just as the apparently neglected grass snake will emerge from the string of egg cells left in the headland midden to be warmed and incubated by the heat of decomposition and the summer sun.

I remember, after finding the nest of the woodcock in the planting, I resolved to keep away in future. It gave me some satisfaction to know that woodcock nested there, just as it did to know where the pied wagtail nested, and the dipper, too. Whether they were the descendants of the original birds or not, woodcock nested in the little wood until it was at last cut down and churned up by the foresters. It is a sad thought that the chain is broken and what had happened before I was born no longer happens there, but here again the pattern applies, and somewhere else the resident birds drop into a wood and make a nesting place beneath a towering tree, and it is unlikely that shooting alone will alter this, so long as there are woods and thickets to the liking of the birds. There are many migrant woodcock still about the woods in February and March, preserved, fortunately, by the game laws which say that they shall not be shot, but perhaps if it were otherwise it wouldn't be long before the residents were killed off and the visiting birds sorely depleted.

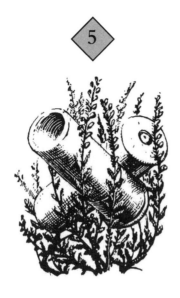

BRUSHES WITH THE FOX

IT was only when I came to live in Wales that I had anything like close acquaintance with the fox. True, I had lived for a short time in a southern county where I had been pressed to settle and join the farmers' hunt, but I had been brought up in a district where the fox was unknown. He had been driven back into the remote hills and if he ventured to trouble anyone, it was the hill shepherd, who had only one way of countering him – total war which included gin traps, poison, shot and the special devices for extracting foxes from inaccessible holes.

The first time I heard a vixen scream was when I lived in a house beside a wooded gully and here, one night when the moon was half shrouded and a hush was upon the sleeping village, I was awakened by the most unearthly sound that seemed to me to have been made by a woman being strangled. I jumped from my bed and stood for a while peering out at the moonlit path among the trees and listening to the sound of the stream. In a little while the vixen screamed again. If murder indeed it was, it was a long drawn-out business and the struggle went on along the ridge above the stream until I heard it again, high up beyond the road, half an hour later. I was ashamed at first that I had done nothing. I could have run off in my night attire to awaken the village policeman and all I had done was to stand by the open bedroom window with my hackles up and my mind in turmoil. When I thought about it afterwards I wondered what the stout old policeman would have said. Had I never heard the vixen in the mating season? Didn't I know that the fox crossed the road and robbed the hen-runs of the village – cocked his leg where the village dogs did the same, and made the rats that scuttled across the street take shelter lest he make an end of them.

I didn't know the fox because he hadn't belonged in my world, a well-keepered country where magpies and crows were almost as well-numbered as the sheep on the hills, and the gibbets advertised themselves for miles as the corpses of rats, stoats, weasels, waterhens, crows, jays, magpies and owls rotted away. I was in the fox's country, his safest redoubt, the rough hinterland of Wales with all its wooded ravines, its rocky hillsides, crags and boulders in which the red one could hide and breed and venture out to take his prey, or sleep the day away in bracken without danger, or the sound of the baying of hounds and the hunter's horn. A fox, they say, will run before hounds a distance of up to sixty miles. How far he ventures in search of a mate would be hard to determine, but the fox, of course, isn't a mere resident of a parish. He moves freely within the bounds of large rivers, natural or man-made barriers or walls and sometimes, if he has a mind to, he swims the river or circumvents the highest walls.

There were fox-hunters in the village, I was to discover, and those who hunted badgers, too. The badger advertises himself much less than the fox by keeping clear of chicken runs (unless he is old and long in the tooth) and trundling along in the side of hedges and along banks where he roots for grubs. The fox, on the other hand, has a natural bent for mischief, a sort of recklessness that suddenly puts him out in the open in the middle of the day with the whole village gasping and pointing and scrambling for weapons, releasing penned dogs, plundering for an old gun and a cartridge.

If I hadn't seen the fox very often in my earlier days, I was due to see him in my new surroundings and have it confirmed that the legend of the fox and the goose is reliable at least in the detail that a fox can carry off the biggest Christmas goose. I am sure this doesn't often happen. Wanton slaughter is in the nature of the fox. He will drop into a pen of fowls and kill and kill, excited to a frenzy of killing by the panic he creates, by the lure of the flapping wings, the blood he has drawn; but he usually kills the first time to feed the family and carry away a hen or a young cock, if he can manage that, without being detected.

Once, however, I discovered a dog-fox that had taken a fine big goose just a day or two before the geese were due to come up for sale in the near-by market This dog-fox had often crossed my path on the way up a wooded gully. More than once he had stopped and looked at me with one paw raised, knowing that he was too far away to be harmed and perhaps sensing that I was there to shoot something much more profitable than a member of his tribe The earth was on the side of a steep grassy slope, concealed by a broom bush, but the goose wasn't taken to the earth. It was carried across a stream – I traced the trail of feathers and knew exactly which farm had suffered the loss – and on into a copse of hazel and bullace trees. Here, under a fallen chestnut of vast proportions, there was an earth of sorts and the fox had backed into the hole dragging the goose with him.

The weather had been cold and he had probably been very hungry, but the dead goose was as well-concealed as a thief could have made it, considering the lack of covering materials. I took a snap shot at a bouncing rabbit that jinked and went in under the chestnut. When I went to recover my kill I found the fox's booty. He had dined in great style. I suppose an old keeper might have poisoned the carcass, but it was no affair of mine. I saluted the fox. He had taken chances, been a little reckless in leaving such a trail, but he hadn't stopped under the chestnut to feed longer than was safe. He had gone off to the earth down along the side of the gully. He could have been ambushed, I think, for I looked in at the mass of feathers and bones twice after that and found that he had been back.

This particular dog-fox was marked down by one of the village fox-exterminators. There was a bounty on the brush of a fox and there were plenty of people ready to spend time hunting one down. I met the man who was after the gully fox one misty afternoon. He was standing in the side of a thorn tree smoking a cigarette. He must have thought very little of the fox's ability to sort out scents associated with man or he would have put away his cigarette. It was the smell of tobacco that led me to him, in fact. I have always been able to pick up such a scent at a great distance and I knew someone was up the rough path ahead of me because the smoke hung in the air. Just where he was I didn't know, but when I had studied the ground I knew he was standing behind the thorn and I guessed he was there because it was the only cover within range of the fox's earth.

'You expect the fox to show?' I asked with a smile. The man with the old gun shrugged his shoulders.

'I'll get him one of these days,' he said.

I suppose he must have spent hours, days perhaps, waiting for that fox. It was months afterwards that he came down the gully one afternoon carrying a fox by the brush.

'There you are,' he said. 'What did I tell you? He came across the top of the gully just now with a young rabbit in his mouth.'

Even an old dog-fox forgets danger and runs carelessly in daylight, sometimes when the earth is too hot or cubs are about and the vixen needing help. This old dog had had his day. His coat was poor, his ears scarred from old battles or love play in the mating season. I couldn't tell which, but he had been killed not by a shot but by a projectile, a trimmed cartridge that had gone out like a shell, the cardboard having been cut through or almost through, just above the brass. How the barrel of that old Damascus gun must have stretched to let such a thing pass through! When it hit the fox, somewhere behind the rib cage, he had died horribly, poor creature. He would have suffered less with a load of B.B. used at the same range. He hadn't been shot. He had been assassinated, in my opinion, and when I looked at his killer I almost wished that the gun had split open and given him the sort of mutilation it had inflicted on poor Reynard.

Often when I went to shoot over the collection of farms on which I had obtained permission I was urged to shoot the fox, but only on one occasion did I ever do so and that was when a poor emaciated fox sprang out to rob me of a rabbit, a most startling happening. The fox had been lying in the underbrush with a gin trap on his leg, frustrated every time he tried to stalk his food by the jingle of the trap's chain until, at last, I had killed before him and he couldn't resist rushing out and risking his life to take my kill. It was a mercy shot. His hind leg was useless and his condition pitiful.

Other foxes I saw on dozens of occasions as they cut across my path, angled up a brow ahead of me or ran the furrows. I could never convince myself that they were near enough to be killed, quickly and cleanly, that the load in my gun was adequate, that they were any more predatory than I was! 'You'll keep an eye open for the old fox, eh?' the farmer would say confidently. I would nod. I kept an eye open for them. I didn't like to see them maimed as they sometimes were. I didn't like to think of them being poisoned and I hated to think of some of the ways they were taken, but I wasn't a shooter of foxes myself, and never could be.

Years later, when we kept hens, I used to wonder how I might react to discovering the Rhode Island-Light Sussex, or the wayward Anconas that loved to roost outside the run, slaughtered by a hungry fox, but no hungry fox came to plague us or put my sentimental heart to the test. There had been a rogue fox on the ground before my time. It had plundered the hen-run and made a name for itself in the locality. Time and again it had escaped by the skin of its teeth, but its nerve had never been shaken. It had become accustomed to hue and cry and panic chases. Perhaps the lesson it had learned was that man kept his head less well than a company of chickens in a moment of alarm. Shot sped over him and past him. He knew where to turn and where to run. He was a master of the art of running in dead ground, anticipating interception. He could lie low. He was as foxy as a fox could be and grew older and more cunning until our predecessor and the farmers round about made a plan to give the alarm and chase him without great haste, to let him have freedom of movement in the open, but stop his bolt holes.

As a result one afternoon in high summer the hour struck. Out he came from the farmyard with the hens cackling and the peace of the drowsy day disturbed; and instead of a great sound of shouting and a clatter of pursuit the farmer picked up the telephone and made a few calls, took down his gun, summoned his helpers and began the hunt in an orderly fashion. The old fox, running for the gate in the hollow, found that the way ahead was blocked, turned back and crossed the open, heading for the hole in the netting in the woodside and discovered that place was manned. In a little while he had run up and down a hedge bank twice and found no way of escape, and the circle closed in, combing the odd clumps of gorse and bramble, watching the open ground until they had him surely inside gunshot from one party or another. When he showed at last he streaked for a bank, his gait a little stiff because of his age, his brush streaming behind him, his ears set back and his fangs bared. They didn't need to shout or run. One of the party calmly stepped out and swung with him as he tried to escape. The gun boomed and he stopped where he was in full gallop, immobilised for ever.

The party gathered and examined him. His brush was dull and lank, the skin of his back and neck was hairless and like tanned leather. He had come to the end of his run. 'The old devil,' they said. How many hundreds of fowls he had taken no one would have cared to say, nor how many so-called good shots he had foiled in his earth-hugging escapes. Someone took the brush for the miserable reward and without the brush he was as pathetic as an old sheepdog. They were sorry for him then perhaps, but they threw him on the stone heap and left him to the big Welsh blow flies, the burying beetles and the warm sun, and he made no more of a nuisance of himself than an old, dead maggotted sheep.

County pest officers often find themselves having to organise fox shoots in the rough upland country in my part of the world, for it is in such places that the breeding stock of foxes becomes well entrenched. Shepherds find signs of the fox and lose numbers of lambs and it isn't long before they are demanding action. They go to look after their flocks with a gun in the crook of their arm, but a gun is a nuisance to a man who has a hard day's work to do and often although he marks the earth in a certain place he hasn't all the tools or the time to do anything about it.

When a fox hunter appears on the scene he is welcomed. They point out to him the general locality, or the exact situation of the earth if they know it, and off he goes with his terriers and his tools. Almost invariably the fox cubs are in an earthen chamber deep under a rock and the terriers are badly mauled if they encounter the vixen. Her bite is always infectious and many a dog is incurably poisoned. The cubs have less formidable teeth. They snarl and tear and back into a corner and the terrier has to be small and agile to drag one out, and strong as well, to secure purchase with back and front legs while this is going on. Often, of course, the struggle is hopeless, a depression in the tunnel, a bend or a jutting boulder defeats the terrier and in the end the foxhunter calls them off and begins to dig.

The Welsh hills are often singularly solid and the hole a fox chooses turns out to have been a fissure into which has fallen the most meagre crumbling of sterile earth and dead fibres. There is no progress to be made with a spade. A pick makes hardly any impression and the earth proves to be one of those dangerous holes in which a dog could easily be entombed if the first boulder should slip a few inches. The remedy is the oldest one ever, adopted by the savage perhaps before he knew how to knap a flint. When a long briar is to be found close at hand, it is uprooted and brought to the earth and poked down the tunnel. Being flexible it will pass the boulders and minor obstacles blocking the way to the chamber in which the cubs are huddled. Once it reaches them it is twisted by the root, turned and turned like a corkscrew until the thorns pick up in the downy coat of the cub. When this happens it is a simple matter to bring the victim up. He must come because he is hooked and held fast.

Sometimes the cubs are far enough down to escape the extreme limits of the briar and there, one might think, the savage is defeated and the law of survival operates, but the fox-hunter knows a thing or two. He comes already equipped for such an eventuality, perhaps, or he goes away and returns with the more certain tool in the shape of a long strand of barbed wire cut from one of the grazing fences. This, when a tight loop is made at one end, serves even better than the briar. As it reaches the place where the cubs are, the outer end is twisted about a bar of wood that will serve to make the whole thing something like a long auger and let it be twisted effectively.

Only the tails of foxcubs need be produced for a bounty payment and no one sees what goes on out on the wild hillside. The battle between terriers and a vixen can be a ferocious and far from one-sided affair. The terriers that are used are the stoutest-hearted little animals that can be found. Often they are old and stiff, sometimes half blind, but they know their work and it is hard to call them off once they join battle down below. On a Sunday a wandering fox-hunter, if he is lucky, may earn a bounty of three or four pounds and a tribe of hill foxes may be eliminated in a few weeks. It is all a rather sad business, for the hill fox finds scant food on the mountain in winter. Lambs may be the prey of the family, but the grazing itself benefits from the fox because he is indefatigable in digging out the voles that simply ruin the turf with their endless labyrinth of tunnels. The buzzard hangs aloft for the same purpose and yet, protected or not, it is blasted without fear of the consequences, because it sometimes plagues a chicken run, where it may be waiting for a rat, but seems to be about to drop on a company of day-olds following the hen.

The hill fox probably has as large a family as any fox in wooded country, but he is generally a leaner animal and shows a considerable variation in colouring at times. The territory the hill fox hunts is extended as the season changes, just as the territory of crows extends. Nevertheless, a given area supports just so many predators and the balance is kept naturally. It is true that a fox may become a parasite on the hill shepherd's flock. Sometimes, early in the season, this is almost inevitable and the protests of the shepherds are loud. No flock master suffers such losses as the hill shepherd. He walks twenty miles or more and thinks nothing of it. He searches for the stragglers of his flock, wades a stream, flounders across a tract of rushes to examine a ewe, only to find that she is past treatment because on an earlier day she eluded him, lying under a great rock. He takes his losses here and there in a variety of ways, a drowned lamb here where it couldn't scramble up the slippery peat bank and slid back, splaylegged to die while its foolish mother watched from above, a couple of ewes and a lamb or two, cragged high on the sheer face of the mountain, starving on a patch of stained grass with no nourishment left in it, and at least one or two every week killed by falling.

The presence of a fox to add to this toll, this natural tythe, is enough to make the shepherd lose his everyday stoicism. He cries out for vengeance. He can do nothing about the carrion crow that drops to the sickly lamb and takes its eye or disembowels it by drawing the umbilical cord and flies off the moment man and dog come over the skyline, but he can bring down his wrath on the fox and when all else fails, take part in a drive to eliminate the nuisance on a particular stretch of the mountain.

The fox shoots that take place under the direction of the county authorities are always properly conducted affairs. No one idly plans to take the time of busy hard-working hill farmers and waste it either by fruitless walking and climbing or by failing to see that the party includes reasonably reliable shots. If the fox is lying out, everything is in his favour, because the mountain is wide and the trails numerous. If he is underground, his living quarters generally have one or more bolt holes and some of these are hard to find and almost impossible to block or cover. John Peel's pack might not guarantee the death of the fox on the mountain, but I doubt whether John Peel hunted to give guarantees and he probably enjoyed seeing the fox beat him on the high fells as much as he enjoyed bringing his quarry to bay.

Hill-fox shoots when they take place are cold-blooded affairs in which, like in great battles, the participants must trust to generalship, for the greater part of the day may be spent in waiting, sitting on a rock on the far side of a ridge with nothing to do but listen for the alarm while the buzzard swings down the hillside or the peregrine calls to his mate somewhere in the face of the crags. I have been present as a spectator more than once. There was an occasion when I was armed with a fly-rod, which I didn't use on the fox, of course!

When the shepherds get together to shoot a fox they are formidable because the fox himself has hardly a more intimate knowledge of the ground. They know the tracks the sheep take as they work their way over the grazing. They know the elephantine rocks, the cathedrals of stone that stand here and there, the streamlets and springs, every rowan tree and every dead tree that marks a slope and every vestige of cover the fox may seek. Few of them are ever marksmen of any consequence, but marksmanship without field knowledge in such cases is hardly an advantage. When the operation is planned, it is planned with more than cunning, and the result, one might think, would be certain.

On the other side of the line is the instinct and fieldcraft of the fox. He has not simply walked the hills. He breathes the air he first breathed when he was whelped. His oneness with the ground is complete. He lives on the mountain as the stunted tree lives there, in spite of all things designed to drive him off and snuff out his life. He is conditioned to danger and when the hunt begins he could run the hill short of most of his senses, listening without seeing, seeing without hearing, taking cover without working out anything but the general direction of the chase, moving fast when he needs to or trotting gently across open ground as slowly as the shadow of a drifting cloud.

There are no sharper eyes than the eyes of a hill shepherd. He has a lifetime of training. He searches the whole mountain for the movement of a grazing sheep, the sight of a lamb far away up among the white quartz and the scree of slate, and when he scans the mountain for the movement of the fox he makes a search worthy of the kestrel or the floating buzzard, with their focusing vision that seems to isolate the field mouse at a height of a hundred feet. The fox's movement allows for this. His greatest danger lies in enemies with training in the field. It is an even contest except that more than one hill shepherd joins the chase and the brigands they bring with them are dotted strategically about the skyline. When the fox hurries for the pass he hurries towards death. The long, shrill whistle of the shepherd gives warning and perhaps up there on the steep face someone cocks the hammers of his gun and prepares himself. It is then only a matter of seconds, of heart-beats, footprints on the sun-dried boulders while the wind blows gently, ruffling a man's hair and slicking back the fox's hackles.

There may be a certain atavistic elation when the report of the gun echoes and reverberates in the cwm or across the valley. A kill stirs the hunting pack. It is the climax of the chase, but it is a sad thing, too, and from my own experience of watching these affairs something darkens the day, takes the brilliance out of the sky. The mountains and the sky reflect in a man's heart just as they do in the moorland pools. There are moments when to be victorious is more depressing than to be defeated and outwitted. This will never be understood by people who are remote and removed from things of the field. There is a world of difference between a hunter and a killer, between the trial of skills and the use of a mechanism designed to exterminate.

Perhaps the strain of my forebears has bequeathed to me something short of the killer instinct, but I don't think this is so. I think that although there are brutal individuals who kill without thinking, there are many thousands of others who, when they reach a particular stage in the contest, would willingly let the quarry run, give him best without being sentimental about the thing, admitting that every animal that lives is sharpened or made dull by his experience or lack of it – the law that governs predators is old and inexorable, and man, whatever he produces from his philosophic study, remains inside the law of survival of the fittest.

I have never ridden to hounds. I am no sort of horseman. I think that hunting is an extravagant way of keeping down foxes and I am not sure that it actually keeps them down. Indeed, some say, it may even foster the fox and result in foxes being planted where there were none before, but without taking up the cudgels of this perennial controversy I would say that the people who make the attack might examine their emotions and decide whether or not they attribute the correct reactions to creatures few of them have studied closely. Is the fly tormenting the trout, does the swallow torment the fly, does the kitten chase the ball of wool because it is playing and do they think that what happens in a locked slaughterhouse, because it is out of sight, makes them less responsible for bloodshed because they garnish their lamb or look the other way? More bloody deeds are done to put meat on plates than are ever seen in a hundred years in the field, but, then, we must have meat! We need not hunt – and there is merit in seeing that no one else does so – it does something for righteousness' sake.

HARE WITHOUT HOUNDS

THE majority of people are familiar with the hare in one form or another. They see enough of them hanging in the poulterer's shop between autumn and Christmas, they know about the March hare or have an inkling that the stuffed device the greyhounds pursue so readily is meant to represent an animal that runs the fields. A few know the hare in its natural element, have heard the legends of its behaviour in March, like to eat jugged hare, or have hare soup.

For me, although I might shoot a hare once in a while and hope that it might be young enough to be jointed and fried, hares have a fascination of their own. That they live above ground sets them apart from the rabbit tribe and that the doe conceals her distributed youngsters and returns to feed them at different times gives the hare a special place, a survival pattern through certain habits that I class with the moorhen's nest-building to anticipate flood. Hares may be mad in March. They may at times display a seeming innocence in the face of danger or they may be downright stupid most of the time, but they, like the hill fox, belong where they choose to live and maintain their numbers on a given territory unless they are driven and decimated by repeated coursing or hare drives.

Perhaps the most endearing thing about the hare is its preference for the open field, the stubble or the pasture, and the way it will lope along a brow regardless of background. It seems to be able to judge the range of danger or its safety zone with considerable wisdom. It keeps a little more than gun range to left, right or centre. It has just the right speed to keep it out of range when casual walkers are crossing the field and it doesn't run into danger until it is seriously alarmed. When it is startled into panic escape, it earns the name of hare-brain. It watches the rear as it rushes headlong into a circling dog or the very mouth of a gun, and then it somehow braces its forelegs, switches its hindquarters round and runs at a different angle. It isn't hard to hit and, unless it is cleanly killed, its cry is heart-rending. That so many hares clutter the game-dealer's rail at times puzzles me. We aren't exactly a hare-eating people. Ask nine out of ten people you encounter what they think of the hare and they will turn up their noses. Jugged hare is a gourmet's dish, or next to it. Hare soup is something most cooks embark upon with reluctance and most diners take with some hesitancy. Mention that it is made with the rich blood of the hare, which now looks something like coffee, and those with weak stomachs begin to toy with their spoons. The flesh of the hare is darker than that of the rabbit, it always seems to me. It couldn't be faked to appear to be chicken. It is very tasty if it has been nicely roasted and garnished and the hindleg of a leveret fried and suitably dressed for the plate is simply delicious. Nevertheless, few people really appreciate the hare and those who do must take their fill when the game-dealer has so many to sell. Presumably he sells them, and to hare-eaters at that, unless there is some chef's trick that makes the hare seem like grouse.

The annual glut of hares apparently arises from a new fashion of holding hare shoots. There was a time when an estate owner would get his keepers together and arrange with them to have a day or two at the hares, if hares were particularly numerous, and keepers have shot hares until carts had to be brought out to cope with the bag. The numbers were considered unworthy of note. The purpose of the exercise was probably to leave the meadows and fields uncluttered with hares that might put birds to flight when serious drives were being held. An old keeper who regularly took part in hare clearance told me last summer that he had once shot hares until his gun got too hot to hold and his master had gone off home, whereat the keepers had simply fired in the air to save themselves the work of splicing the bag and loading them on the carts. In those far off days, the hare thrived and maintained its great numbers — as it is still doing. Today it seems that in many parts of the country the hare has come on because the rabbit has declined, and whether it eats exactly the same herbage as the rabbit or not, farmers prefer to see it shot, hence the great bags of hares that result from drives arranged during the game season.

Hares are at their best when the ground is hard. They are much easier to see, as is the case with all ground game, when the bracken has finally slumped, the roots are in, the hedges are stripped of their thicker undergrowth and the leaves are blowing. A hare drive has its excitements, nevertheless, because hares will hug the ground until they are compelled to run once the shoot is on, and they have a habit of skulking in a patch of round rushes or hanging in a hollow to make a run at the last minute. Their take-off is often a very noiseless affair. They are a wonderful blend with their background, brown as the rusted bracken, fawn to match the dead stubbles, the dried-out feathery grass, dark on the back so that they look like the blackthorn hedge, rufous on the neck like the red dock leaf. At once they belong to the plough and the stubble, the bracken, the wood and the bank, and their speed is designed somehow to deceive the eye. Perhaps the smoothness of the movement of the running hare is the most camouflaging thing about it. There are times when the creature is a ghost, a running shadow with indistinct outline, and there are times when this fact misleads the man who suddenly becomes aware that he has put one up.

Taking them all in all, however, no sort of hare presents any great difficulty to the man with the gun. They are all tall in the leg. They may appear to hug the slope as they gallop up it, but they are well clear of the grass. They don't carry shot well although many a hare taken at extreme range appears to do so. Those who walk after hares have found that the far-out hare that seemed to be running well and getting away unscathed as likely as not dropped after half a mile or perhaps a mile.

If there is a place to shoot a hare, give me a rough bogland with uneven ground and numerous tracks through the round rushes. This sort of terrain gives the hare and the shooter an even chance. In a wood the hare often runs and stops and appears to have no sense of danger, taking comfort, perhaps, from the canopy of branches overhead, but in a rough bit of ground or among watermeadows the hare has his runs, his cover and his campaign, and while the dogs work forward he can choose his moment to cross the hump, jump the feeder and head for the hole in the hedge. When he tumbles head over heels after being

driven forward towards escape routes, he may prove a cumbersome addition to the game bag, but he is a worthy adversary.

Hare coursing is something that can hardly be called hunting the hare. It is an exercise in the handling of greyhounds, a sort of platoon exercise for men funnelling the hares across the flat fields to provide a trial for handlers and greyhounds. It is an occasion for all the eager, red-faced country folk who love equally the meet, the point-to-point and the pony race, and whose forebears stood at the pit to see the gamecocks matched. Whatever happens to the hare is a side issue and while many a hare is tumbled, many a one escapes to run another day. The book-making world don't take bets on the hare. It is unfortunate that an electric hare couldn't be rigged to perform as the live one does. It is also unfortunate that the greyhound, handsome and fleet though it may be, isn't really an efficient animal in the business of hare-hunting. The whippet does much better and the lurcher better still. I once hunted hares with dogs – not hounds, for I have no experience of beagles – and discovered that the ideal combination was a fleet of foot dog that could turn the hare and a slower, more deliberate dog that could make the kill neatly and cleanly.

I am convinced that the upland hare and the hare of the meadows have distinct characteristics and limit their movements to their own sort of territory. The upland hare likes the fine grasses that the mountain sheep browses upon. It haunts the cover of birch and rowan tree and has its form in the fern and bracken. It is a slighter, less heavy animal and its colouring suits the brown hill, while the hare of the arable field, the river plain and the seaboard is generally larger, thicker in the back, heavier in the flanks and likes the cover of rushes, reeds, long grass runnels and man-made banks that contain ditches and streams. A good bog hare will weigh a full eight pounds, while an upland hare will run a pound or two less. The upland hare will have a greater turn of speed and rely on his ability to run, while the bog hare moves more ponderously in the potato field, the kale, the tall weeds and the scrub and undergrowth that clogs the uncultivated land close to river or pond.

On the open field, the plough or the stubble, the hare is an incidental to be taken when one walks to put up a partridge covey or flush a skulking cock pheasant. As an incidental item shot in the course of a casual excursion, the hare that is put up from his bed on a bright sunny morning in October or November may give one a certain reassurance that one's eye is still in; and the swinging shot at a hare running upwards across a slope is sometimes a test for a man with a gun. Give him time, follow through, shoot without excitement. All these little bits of advice may run through one's head if suddenly, for the first time in years, one finds a hare within range. And the hare isn't hard to hit. He really is a big target and nothing like as fast as a snipe or a teal razoring away towards the rising sun; but people miss hares. They miss them because the hare is big, because of a feeling that a large object is easily hit, because they know that a bouncing rabbit kicked out of a gorse bush goes faster, and because that smooth movement, that racehorse quality that makes the hare seem unhurried, is deceiving. I am ashamed when I miss a hare and perhaps more ashamed because when I try to shoot one I have made the decision to shoot. Most of the time I prefer to let the hare run. Like many another feat I have tested myself and found I can do it without undue strain.

The hare's fascination, so far as I am concerned, has something to do with its background and natural behaviour, as I have said, but it also has its legends. It behaves in a very odd way in March and the mating season. It dances on its back legs, it indulges in running battles, it appears to be blind to danger. It is as mad as a hare in March can be and its behaviour has become a by-word. Some years ago a lady, whose word I had no reason to doubt, wrote to me about March hares saying that she had a large doctored cat that was challenged and did battle with a hare every spring, the hare coming down to a field behind her house and dancing on his back legs to spar with the cat. The cat was always outboxed and the hare would then take himself off. How blind a hare must get in the mating season, to mistake a black cat for his own species! I often wondered if this hare was always the same one or if other hares presented themselves to challenge the impotent cat, but I was never able to find out.

The hare legend that has a more sinister ring is the one that tells of the hare being possessed by the witch. This takes its rise, I have no doubt, from the strange, almost human screams emitted by a dying hare. Anyone who has heard a stricken hare's screams will know how disturbing they can be. Like the scream of the vixen, they have an uncannily human quality. In the half-light of a misty October evening who would not be persuaded that he had shot not a hare but a witch who had assumed the form of a hare? Inevitably someone discovered that after he had killed a hare and heard its cry an old woman in the village had died. Perhaps this happened more than once in several places. The witch in the hare's form is larger than the common hare – a hare on the skyline at nightfall always seems bigger and there are times when everything is magnified by the moisture in the air! If no one has died in the village how is the person who shot the hare to be sure that some old woman, in the next village or the one beyond that, didn't depart this life at that very same instant? Every hare that runs at twilight is likely to be bewitched. It is a well-known thing. Say what you like, the scream is human and somewhere an old woman is dying. Ask around, watch the obituary notices in the local paper, remember that the old folk knew what they were talking about!

I must admit that more than once, coming home from a vigil in the wood, with half a dozen pigeons hung at my waist, I have put up my gun and swung to a loping hare and thought again about shooting it, but most of the time I have been thinking not about witches but the reception I might get when I presented pigeons to be plucked as well as a big hare to be paunched and drained of his blood. Old Miss Dunbar, who looked like a witch and lived in a cottage at the end of the road, died before I began to shoot hares. She was probably hurried out of this world by one of the local poachers or someone on his way to the river to flight the duck! To be sure one should shoot a hare in the morning sun, on the long-shadowed fields at sunrise in autumn. Witches, like bats, confine their activities to the half-light and no one who wants to be sure of a hare should put up a gun at one when the light of day is fading. There are fewer witches about these days, of course, and it may be that towards the end of some of the big drives when the figures are running into the hundreds a lot of promising witches are cut off in their prime. It is a subject for consideration.

We have a plague of hares here in Wales at the moment of writing. Never were so many hares to be seen both on lowland and upland farms; the absence of the rabbit is said to have resulted in the hare's flourishing. Hares may be shot all the year round, although they may not be offered for sale during the close season for ground game. The Ground Game Act allows a farmer to destroy the hares that may plague him without reference to the shooting tenant or the owner, but hereabouts few small farmers have much time or the inclination for shooting, and the plague. One wonders if the hare will hold second place to the wood-pigeon as an agricultural pest or if the rabbit will creep back again in time to oust them both, as well it might. Hares never held their own against the rabbit because, although the fully grown hare was a match for the buck, the young hare was invariably ill-used by the latter and stood no chance against him.

The blue hare, one should mention, is less of a gourmet's dish than the brown hare. It doesn't find a place on the rail with hare and grouse and ptarmigan. It is a smaller species of hare than the common sort and some people call it the variable hare and some the mountain hare, variable because it changes its colouring when the equinox is past, or round about that time, and blends better with its background on that account. A brown hare on a snow-covered mountainside is much more conspicuous than one that blends with the snow.

Blue hares are shot, but I have never been able to decide exactly why. They are stringy creatures for any cook to put on the table and they are often pitifully thin, mere bags of sinew and bone. I have never taken the trouble to sample more than one, so perhaps I am no authority on the subject of the blue hare as a course on the menu. I imagine if a man happened to have nothing better to roast over his fire he might be glad of the blue hare, or even the wild mountain goat which eats much the same sort of things and keeps to the same barren places. Leave them, I say, to feed the buzzard or the eagle, to provide something for the feral cat or the vixen's litter.

They are local in the sense that they frequent the high ground and, as far as I know, are absent from places south of Derbyshire, although they may once have run the mountains of Wales. They are, nevertheless, as much a part of the north country as its people and they were probably here when the first man landed, providing food for the wolf as well as the eagle. When wild cats screamed on every mountain and the wolf haunted the scrub trees, the mountain hare was hunted hard I have no doubt. That it has survived so long in difficult country is probably the cause of its sinews and thongs taking up so much room in its miserable body. It kicks up the snow and spurts away across the mountain, tempting the man who has walked a painful mile or two for his wild red grouse to take a shot at the bouncing outline, but in its natural surroundings it does no harm. In my humble opinion it is one of the wild things that might well be left alone. Perhaps someone will make a case to the contrary and suggest that by shooting the blue hare things are made harder for the vermin, but that, I think, would be stretching things.

PIGEONS
AND PIGEON TACTICS

◇◇

THERE is no doubt that now the rabbit's numbers have been
so drastically reduced following the plague, a lot of people, who
asked no more than an odd day kicking out a few rabbits, have
taken to pigeon shooting. Keepers were never too keen on rabbit
shooters (other than the tenant or his appointed representative),
but they couldn't always make an issue of it, although the professional trapper could be watched and checked. The woodpigeon
is just as much of a pest today as the rabbit once was, but unfort-

unately it likes the covers, the very woods and thickets in which game shelters and breeds. Everyone may want to shoot pigeons, but estate owners are hardly likely to welcome a suggestion that their preserves be invaded and their game scattered while the farmer's enemies are killed.

The result of overlapping interests has produced woodpigeon clubs that accept the control of the keepers. Accordingly they are forced to confine their dates to periods when shooting isn't going on and before the breeding stock needs peace to find nesting places. Most clubs that operate in a given area have to arrange things so that particular woods are not overshot and members are able to shoot altogether perhaps twelve times between late November and the end of March. Depending on the district, the bags vary, but in my experience most club shoots are generally more noisy than effective and far too often the birds filter away to unmanned places or to the odd island of trees, the owner of which emphatically refuses to have disturbed. Even more futile is the result when a club shoots on its far boundary without making a date with the adjoining club!

There are pigeon shots and pigeon shots, and for every competent performer the club will have one or even two excitable characters who have no idea how to make use of background, how to judge their range, keep the white outline of their faces from warning incoming birds long before they can be taken, or, in fact, how to do the very thing for which the club has come out. The reason for this hopeless state of affairs often lies with the organisers, who see every new member as a 'body' to be stationed somewhere and make a noise, keeping the birds in the air and circulating. This may be the result, but once pigeons are alarmed by erratic shooting they tend to fly high and turn quickly and even the magnum in the hands of the expert can only reach out so far, while dozens of birds may be peppered and pricked without otherwise being affected.

To make a serious business of pigeon shooting one must shoot alone or in the company of no more than one or two friends. Pigeons have their flight lines and their behaviour pattern in different conditions of weather. They come high over a certain place when the wind is from a particular direction. Their line of approach may vary a little on different days. There are times when they come in droves, bent on suicide, and times when their sight seems keener than ever. These variations are connected with the strength of the light and the general temperature. Like most creatures the pigeon is wild and alert in cold, hard weather, eager for the shelter of the conifers on the approach of snow, a little heavy and confused in the mist of rain that may come before nightfall, and not at all fast when it has been raining all day.

People who talk about shooting pigeons are apt to have a general rule about what constitutes a sound performance – so many cartridges expended per bird. A good shot, they say, will show one bird for every three cartridges, or one for four or five. A good shot intent upon making a bag can shoot with the greatest caution and come near to bagging one for one – or make certain of his bag by killing his birds as they come to perch. A sporting shot may snap at every reasonable bird that passes, whether it curls back, jinks through the tips of trees or breaks from a flight and goes back at top speed, and he may show one bird for five or six cartridges on his good day and one for seven or eight on a bad day.

There is no doubting the fact that the best way to make a bag is with decoys, by laying out and lofting, by building a hide or using bales of straw and some camouflage netting. The professional does this. He wouldn't think of making only sporting shots. He couldn't afford such luxury for one thing! The object of the exercise in his case is to shoot and make it pay. A pigeon may bring half a crown to the dealer, but it isn't worth a lot more than the price of the best cartridge with maximum load so far as the shooter is concerned and the man with the decoys may well be using the little Impax or cheaper ammunition if he can come by it.

To become a fair hand at pigeons one must concentrate. There are good all-rounders, first-class game shots to whom grouse, pheasant, snipe, mallard or pigeon come alike, but even they would admit that their skill at high pheasants, for instance, has been achieved by shooting high pheasants. Their way of trimming the flighting teal didn't suddenly come at the first occasion, even though all other things – gun-fitting, situation, opportunity and so on – were equal. The pigeon has something to teach most of us. It behaves differently at different times, and presents even the expert with a fair test of his skill.

To make a right and left at pigeons may be easy enough when the flight comes streaming in to the larches on a broad front and seemingly oblivious to danger. It isn't quite so easy when one or two pigeons, already rattled by the sound of gunfire on the far side of the wood, sweep over on fast reconnaissance and split their formation at the last minute, turning a wing and diving away to head for the other side of the country. One may debate exactly what a right and left means when flighting. To my mind, it means quite simply to have, after two shots, two dead birds falling at the same time. A lot of people have done this and some have bettered it, but a lot more haven't. The pedants will point out that a right and left is a right and left. But it is possible to shoot a bird with the right barrel and another with the left having in the meantime picked up the first and set it up as a decoy!

I have shot on dozens of occasions in the company of a very fine pigeon shot, who makes his double quite effortlessly and with breath-taking smoothness and never counts his kills or checks his figures. When asked he shrugs his shoulders and looks at his bag. He never knows how he has done, only that he has enjoyed himself. On the odd occasion when I have called to him after making a hopeless right and left, he has obliged by stopping one of the birds I have missed, but invariably – and with amazing modesty – he assures me that the bird was wobbling. I had it. It was coming down anyway. If I am counting I should take it in!

In recent years I have done a lot of pigeon shooting. Bags in

Wales are never particularly high. At club shoots an odd member may claim twenty birds or twenty-five. On rare occasions someone may get as many as fifty, but in this part of the world, where the woods hang on the hillsides, the valleys are small and steep, and the fields only a few acres in size, pigeons tend to be hard to come by and move in comparatively small flocks. I have made good bags shooting solo. I have waited for the flight in a small wood and shot like a master – and I have come home almost empty-handed, too! If I wanted to show a bag I should pick my ground and carry decoys, shooting in the morning and afternoon and perhaps taking to the woodside before dusk. I used to carry a decoy or two and set them out in the stubbles, among the corn stooks or on fields where young peas had been sown with the grain.

The decoy, some people say, need be no more than a silhouette. It can be cut out of tin or hardboard. It can be set up to give a 'plan' view of the feeding bird, or lofted to give a silhouette. The more elaborate decoys one sees in the dealer's window have colour to match the living bird. They are lifelike; they sometimes bob in the breeze. They are light, without shine, and perfect in every way as are the trout flies one may sometimes buy in the same shop. I am inclined to think that decoys are rather like fishing flies. One must give some thought to the natural, but it is unnecessary to copy exactly, to attempt to duplicate nature's own, because exact imitation is the result of a natural process and no man living can match the real thing. My favourite decoy was made of wire and an old waistcoat lining that happened to be exactly the right colour for the job. It brought the birds in because it was right so far as its essential dimensions were concerned. It looked like a pigeon from the side and from above, and I could rely on the birds coming in to it – providing I set it out in a likely place.

Putting out decoys is no problem when one has taken the trouble to study the feeding pattern, but if one goes casually to decoy and initiate birds to drop to a given place. the business depends on instinct for a suitable place. Decoys set out in a particular field may keep a lonely vigil if just out of sight there is a field of clover or newly sown wheat or oats, and the same may be the case when all they depend upon is an odd bird catching sight of them as it rises high over the wood. There is a limit, too, so far as the dimensions of the field go and the height of the surrounding trees. It is far easier to decoy to a reasonably open place, although the open field presents its problem so far as the hide is concerned. Not every field has a couple of bales of hay at hand or a dead thorn lying on the headland. A great deal can be done with a bit of camouflage netting and one or two old sacks and a stick or two, but the foxhole sort of hide has to be carefully sited.

The extraordinary thing about pigeons is that they hardly ever shy at the sketchy hide that looks in-keeping with the general topography, but they keep clear of the painstakingly built affair that completely conceals its occupant, perhaps because it looks out of place. Their sight is as keen as any bird of the field. Some people who set up newly shot birds as decoys are so convinced of this that they trim the eyelids from the decoys although this is perhaps carrying things to an extreme. The essence of a good hide is one that blends with the background, fits the contour, the hedges and bushes, and doesn't come apart at the seams when a quick shot is taken at the departing birds after one has been shot on the ground.

This is always one of the problems for a man who uses a hide and likes a sporting shot. The man who wants to make a bag tries to keep his mind on the business and reminds himself that if he shoots and stays concealed the birds come back more readily than if he steps out to use a second barrel. The number of decoys is a matter of choice. It is true that, as with wet-fly fishing, one will do, but two create a better illusion, and three make a crowd, four or five a company. On a brown field one decoy is a very inconspicuous thing and two not nearly enough, while even one on a stook will serve so long as flocks are about to supplement the layout as and when targets present themselves.

The equipment of a decoyer should consist of some kind of face-covering. Having a fair beard I have no great problem here, but it helps to have some kind of screen for one's face, to break up the outline of a round head perched on square shoulders, to darken the hands or wear mitts and, of course, to have the making of a hide or blind, a sack in which to carry a groundsheet, the decoys, the camouflage net and a support or two. Equipped in this fashion it is a pity to set things out in any but the most fruitful locality. Like pike fishing, it is a solitary pastime and one requiring patience and alertness. Birds have a habit of coming in when they are least expected, sometimes after they have been over and circled and gone away again and always, in my experience, when time hangs heaviest.

There was a time when cheap cartridges could be obtained for pigeon shooting, but for some time now the authorities have discontinued the subsidy. Perhaps they were being pennywise and pound-foolish or perhaps they had themselves been at some of the Brock's Benefit club shoots that used to take place! Cartridges are the test of a man's enthusiasm when they come at from fourteen to twenty shillings a box.

No one who takes up pigeon shooting to recover his expenses can hope to do so unless he uses decoys. The question of making a thing pay may be frowned upon, but the economics of sport are something that few people can overlook. Many a man who wouldn't dream of relating outlay to returns still endeavours to make arrangements with his game dealer – and not always because he has fifty brace of birds to offer – and there are sound sportsmen who fish like fanatics at the beginning of every season in order to make the rent. There are also many farmers who can't afford to shoot the pigeons that plague them because they haven't the time, the ability or the knowledge, and many a frustrated gun finds a way of keeping his eye in as a result!

The pigeon's place as public enemy number one is not in dispute now. It survives so successfully because it feeds on such a variety of food. It takes acorns, ivy berries, wheat, peas, winter cabbage and broccoli of all kinds. It stuffs itself with clover or the bread and cheese of the thorn bush. It is never at a loss even although it must sometimes tax its digestion. The flavour of pigeons varies according to their diet. They are always nice when they have been feeding on stubbles, but ivy berries, which are sometimes their iron rations, hardly improve their flavour! Add to their omnivorous ability the fact that the woodpigeon nests and lays over the longest period of almost any of our native birds and may have young half-fledged in November, or a pair of eggs in the first days of March, and the bird's permanent place in the woods is easily understood.

When times become hard they flock and move away to better feeding localities. They migrate from one part of the country to another and there is a school that claims to be able to recognise a 'foreign' woodie or Scandinavian immigrant, a darker bird than the native. That darker pigeons are to be found, most shooters have noted. For a long time I used to mark them down as newly-arrived birds from across the North Sea. They were generally held to be newcomers, but some years ago I was intrigued to read the results of research by a gentleman well qualified to express an opinion on the dark pigeons. He had found that the dark birds were tubercular. Every bird with dark plumage that was subjected to post-mortem was found to be infected with tuberculosis! Perhaps the close-breeding of woodpigeons brings this about? I believe that it also applied in the case of rabbits in heavily infested districts.

While a lot of people would be delighted to think that the pigeon might be plagued as the rabbit ultimately was, there are others who would poison the birds if they could. The problem that confronts the would-be poisoners is that the pigeon eats what the pheasant eats and, quite apart from the ground game, a lot of useful birds might be drugged at the same time.

A 'selective' pigeon poison has yet to be devised and in the meantime, quite apart from the jolly times that would-be pigeon shooters may have, the farmer faces his losses and wonders what measures might be taken to reduce the pest to reasonable proportions.

Keepers relentlessly poke out and destroy the nests of magpies and carrion crows. This operation doesn't disturb the game overmuch. Pigeons could be reduced in the same way. Such methods are wearisome, but destroying nests whenever and wherever they are found would help a great deal. The half-grown young are said to be very enjoyable, although I have never tasted their flesh. When the parents have just about decided to start a new family, the fledglings are full-breasted and fat. All the predators of the wood that are capable of reaching the nest are on the alert for them. Perhaps we are missing a delicacy! On the other hand, when the farmer's problem has been solved will not the pressure increase in some other direction?

Among the flocks of woodpigeons that trail from wood to wood in late autumn as well as in independent flights, parties of stock doves are often encountered. The habitat of the stock dove is even more varied than that of the woodpigeon, for it may be found in the parkland, on the limestone cliffs in the territory of the more restricted rock dove, and out in the open country.

The stock dove is a finer bird and smaller than the woodpigeon, while the rock dove has a white rump and the stock dove is grey rumped. Stock doves, perhaps because they are smaller and lighter than the woodpigeon, always seem to me to have a better turn of speed when alarmed. This may be simply imagination on my part. The homing pigeon owes something of its ancestry to the rock dove and maybe a little to the stock dove, too, and the homer has that high performance in its initial flight, so perhaps there is something in it, even if feeding and conditioning make a racing bird what it is. The stock dove seems to have a vulnerability to the odd pellet far outside the pattern. It may be that the quills aren't so strong or the down so thick as that of the woodpigeon, and the stock dove doesn't turn the shot on that account; but on occasion, stepping out from a sheltering tree, I have mistakenly shot a stock dove and then noticed one that I hadn't tried for dropping out of the flight perhaps half a mile away.

The stock dove's exact place in the pigeon pattern is a little obscure. They are local and they are often noted only when one is found in the bag, especially when shooting has been fast and furious just before dusk. All cats are grey by night and the stock dove is often seen to be what it is when it is counted. The shooter looks at the smaller bird, notes the metallic sheen on the neck and head, the touch of green perhaps, and the dove grey. It always saddens me just a little to find that I didn't take time to spot the stock dove among the swirling birds trying to slip into the tall trees. The little turtle dove purrs in the thicket and advertises the height of summer, soothing the man who lies on his back looking at the sky. The woodpigeon claps its wings and sails out of the larches. The stock dove makes a harsher sound, but altogether he is undistinguished until one has him in hand, and until then looks no better than the railway-terminus pigeon that runs before the taxi's wheels and perkily mounts the pavement. Could the stock dove fairly be classed as a pest when the wood-pigeon outnumbers it so heavily?

We come to the problem that confronts the fowler – observation and the cultivation of one's powers of recognition. In honesty we must admit that it is a very poor excuse to say that we don't recognise a species. The lesser pigeons can be as easily singled out until the light fades, but again like the wildfowler, we are in a quandary that may deprive us of a shot.

Why, in any case, should the stock dove be spared? The stock dove and the rock dove are by no means as numerous as the woodpigeon and they are genuine natives. They belong where they are found. For my own part I try to distinguish the ring dove from the stock dove on every possible occasion. I wouldn't shoot the rock dove if I could avoid doing so any more than I would set out to destroy racing birds, although I know people with large acres of market garden who have been plagued into shooting everything and anything that attacks their produce, including pheasants, in and out of season!

Talking about rock doves reminds me of my father telling of the days when, as a boy, he kept homing pigeons and scaled the rocks near his home to secure eggs in order to strengthen his breeding strain. The cross-breeding presented no difficulty, but of course an important factor was being overlooked. Continual breeding and rejection of birds weak on the 'homing' side produces birds that can be relied upon to return to the loft no matter what happens. The wild strain is totally deficient in this characteristic unless they home to a particular crevice in a cave, and soon my father found that he was stocking the rocks along the shore and giving the little blue rocks an odd touch of colour here and there without changing his own stock at all!

Feral pigeons are what time and circumstance have made

them. Darwin may have reached profound conclusions through breeding pigeons, but as far as I am aware he never entered a bird for a race and few small boys, or experts for that matter, breed winners with a generation out of a cave!

The neat little rock dove is surely a hardy bird. It survives on the rocky coast, lives on ledges where the wind forces it hard against the rock face, fights its way out through the spume and spray, tossed by the ferocity of the gale, buffeted by freak currents and carried away like leaves in a storm. This says a lot for the ancestors of the homing pigeon. The normal hazards of field and wood are trial enough for the ring and the stock dove, but the rock dove must face a special set of enemies – the hook-beaked great gull, the stooping peregrine, the sharp-eyed carrion crow, the crag-hunting cats, the insidious ways of the stoat working the ledges and scuttling from one island of fine grass to the next.

Is there anything quite so delightful as the sight of a flock of rock doves spread out across the water as they depart from some deep cave overhanging the green waves? There are people who secrete themselves on the shore to shoot rock doves. A great deal of senseless shore shooting goes on, quite apart from what passes for wild-fowling. The sad thing about it all is that rarely is there anyone to raise a protest and when the rock doves are brought down not a few fall in the water or drop in inaccessible places. When the bag is gathered I doubt if it justifies the effort, for a rock dove is a poor picking and about as suitable for the table as one of the Trafalgar Square pigeons.

In my part of the world the rock dove nests not more than a mile from the place in which I live. The 'pigeon hole' is well known. From time to time I hear of youths going to shoot the birds as they go in and out. The same young sportsmen shoot the cormorant and anything else that comes within range. There seems no hope for us when this sort of thing goes on, but the irresponsibility is not entirely confined to the unenlightened. It is irresponsible for us to continue to do nothing about laying down a code of conduct for every man or woman who uses a gun, and a positive penalty for infringement – the taking away of the right to use a gun in future!

DUCK SHOOTING DAYS

ALWAYS when it rains in the evenings of autumn I find a sort of nostalgia overtaking me because I made my first serious expedition after duck on such an evening, a solitary outing, dangerous and lonely, but with all the fascination of the marsh and its surroundings in fading light, all the mystery of creeping mists and the hushed closeness of moisture-laden atmosphere. The marsh was a haunted place at the best of times, for its stunted and dead trees had grotesque outlines that suggested rearing devils and covens of consulting witches. It gripped the imagination whether one might be poet, hunter or both. Its main watercourse was almost undefined by distinguishable banks, but there was a main watercourse somewhere beyond the carpets of green weed, the stands of rushes, the treacherous pile of interwoven waterlilies and lances of reed, islands of stones and shoulders of black peat. In this wilderness there were tortuous paths that led nowhere unless to the brink of pits, in the depths of which one looked to see a great green pike or speckled trout, but saw instead the distorted outline of the ribs or backbone of some beast that had ventured too close and left its bones to gather a coating of fine silt.

Out in the centre of the marsh there was life in plenty, the clattering, splashing life of companies of waterfowl that chased each other round secret pools and hidden bays or travelled in little flotillas sending eddies running to the reeds in their wake. The main watercourse was in fact a shrunken loch, a sort of meandering, slow river, an almost imperceptible current carrying drifting feathers towards the outflowing stream away at the neck of the marsh. A fowler's world, I was to learn, is full of enchantment of this sort, of peace and magic, a fleeting wonder to be seen in the streak of dawn dividing the low shadows from the frowning of the night, a western flare that is the quenching of the sun on a horizon a thousand miles away, it seems, and then the growing of night and shadow and the coming of the flight.

All this I came to know in time, but here, with the owl crying, a dog barking in some farmyard where night was settling and the waterfowl talking, I became possessed. I was no longer aware of my normal background, but bereft of recollection of the family's faces, the sound of the ticking clock, the warmth of the peat fire. All this had evaporated. I made my first steps in the marsh without looking back, without thinking that there was a way back or that the chill of rain becomes more intense when darkness is complete, that thorns would pluck at my coat and scratch my hands and water would overflow my boots, shocking me with the sudden coldness that would shortly – in a month or less — stop the weeds and make them sink back into the peaty water.

Duck were beginning to flight and I had come for that. I could see them to the west, against the lighter sky. I caught glimpses of them when they appeared above the barrier of the alders, the ancient willows, blackthorns and dead, barkless birches. I had studied the place a hundred times, of course, and I had followed the tracks of hare and the slots of deer, but only with my eyes. I had been tempted to venture out there by the spirits of the place, but the spell had never overcome me completely, for I had cautiously thought about the treacherous peat that looked firm but was no more than an outer crust of a bottomless mass of decomposing material that now and then, in summer, gave a belch of marsh gas and bubbled like a cauldron.

People, I sometimes think, are inclined to be like birds in their social conduct. Some are gregarious and some solitary, the gregarious enjoying themselves in concerted activity, chattering like monkeys, quarrelling like springtime rooks about the rookery, and the solitary conducting themselves like fishing herons or sailing buzzards. To say that I come within the latter category may be to admit that my schoolmasters failed and there was some deficiency in my tribal training, but I have always preferred my own company fishing or shooting.

There are times, I will not deny, when I have wished that I had company at hand, but the drawbacks are for me always outnumbered by the advantages of simplified decisions and responsibilities. One wades into deep water with the knowledge that no one else is compelled to share the risk or needs to be told or warned. The private world of the man who travels alone has immense compensations quite apart from the fact that wolves and jackals hunt in packs and mass courage is usually hysteria.

None of these things had formulated in my mind, of course.

I had as yet no time for philosophy. I found myself out in the deep marsh with the light of departing day above me and mallard moving closer and closer to the position I had taken behind the leafless thorn. There was, and would be again and again in the future, something so absorbing in my situation that I had thought for nothing but the moment I was living. It was the same as remaining in the depths of the hills by the side of some secret water, waiting for the fish to rise, seeing the start of the boil of rings, and hearing the fish suddenly feeding all round me.

The first mallard that came within range flew at eye-level right out of the blackness of the distant trees, away beyond the reeds. All at once it was there, clear of the background, growing in size and coming fast, and desperately I tried to get perspective and judge distance before it came right through me. I put up the gun and covered it. It was there in front of me and it came on after I fired, but there was an instant when I knew the wings weren't propelling it and then a second later it crashed into the thorn tree making me duck.

I had begun to make my bag and all at once the marsh was alive, full of the sound of wings and disturbed water, erupting fowl that burst from reeds and sprang from pools, or ran the surface to make a paddling take-off. They swirled over the black trees, swept low over the far-out watercourse, mounted into the whiter sky and went into the mist to skim the hidden cornfield, skirt the pastures and the scrub trees and come back in again in the cover of drifting rain. I stood wondering how I might retrieve the next bird I shot. I had no dog, no water spaniel or burly labrador to plunge through the water-holes for me. I was about to commit the first serious folly of the inexperienced fowler, to shoot things I couldn't recover and might never find, or to venture where no one but a fool would set foot in daylight, let alone in darkness.

When the alarm had passed and the fowl were swinging down here and there to alight again, the wary drakes keeping high and far out while the less cautious birds settled, I stood close to the thorn and prepared myself as a small flight crossed to my left and swung round again, circling my position. The bird I selected was high and he stood there, halted for an instant before he plummeted down and I heard him strike the bog. I had two duck, or so it seemed, and had fired only two cartridges, although a moment later a duck that had blundered in and spotted me razored away at great speed and made me miss, reducing my elation. There was no way that I could persuade myself that I had him and that if I hadn't seen him fall he had actually travelled a long trajectory to drop on the edge of a pool three hundred yards away, because he had made no such curving flight. He had gone up and away, deep into the night sky, erased from my sight by the blanket of mist and rain that hung over the whole marsh.

They didn't come back so quickly or so close to my thorn tree and for a little while it seemed to me that my three shots had given every duck on the marsh my exact position. Those in flight had marked the direction of the sound and were keeping away and those afloat had judged the range. This is perhaps one of the minor drawbacks of shooting alone. It is impossible to discover where the fowl have settled or whether they have gone beating round gathering their stragglers before moving away to more peaceful waters, although in areas not often disturbed it is generally a case of birds settling in places from which they can keep watch or know of old that approach is impossible. Sooner or later, however, when a place is a well-visited feeding ground or base for excursions to near-by stubbles, fowl begin to move again in regular lines of flight.

My fourth shot was wild, but my fifth brought a drake tumbling away to my right and splashing down into a water-hole.

When I had shot a fourth I looked at the sky and the gathering shadows among the trees and decided to pick what I had shot, carrying my gun with me and keeping an eye open for an odd duck getting its bearings in the gloom. I could see the second duck I had shot. It stood on the peat, a wing showing its underside and the remainder a dark shadow, but I was blackened to the thigh before I grabbed it and my gun barrels had dipped dangerously towards the black ooze. I knew that the third and fourth were going to be difficult. In time I would know that no fowl that flies drops out in a treacherous bog to be anything else but a lure, to entice the hunter and bury him in green weed or the porridge of saturated peat. I tied my drake to my waist and began to wade.

The difference between daylight and night had gone, nor was it twilight in which one could see a flickering bat had bats been on the wing. Fowl fly in the dark and the owl, too, but darkness closes tighter about a fowler than it does about the echelon of water-birds. I was waist-deep in heaving bog before I had gone five yards and the awful fear struck me that going on was the same as going back and standing still was to go down, slowly, like a trapped beast. The white feathers of the bird I had shot sailed about me as I tried to stride forward. I held the gun high, but the tails of my coat were afloat. Soon I would be swimming and the trees out there would rise higher. I was young. I began to think that all the warnings I had about flighting duck hadn't been the old wives' tales I had considered them to be!

It is sometimes said that fortune favours the brave and something protects the trusting and the innocent. I am inclined to think that people often escape their just desserts in order that experience may be seared into the species, that the process of conditioning to environment may go on and ultimately the fit may survive. Call it, for simplification, the hand of Providence – or luck. The man who doesn't live to tell his tale leaves no reliable lesson for his fellows, but the child who burns his fingers hardly ever needs warning again. I came by accident on the third of my bag and took it with me. It was part of the purpose of my venturing into the depths. I floundered and struggled towards a bush because it seemed that where a bush grew the foothold would be better, but the bush proved to be the flourishing top of a straggling and submerged tree through which I struggled and clambered, disentangling the tied duck from twigs and sticks as I went, and praying that when I got through the obstacle, the ground would be firmer and the water more shallow.

This proved to be the case. On the far side of the submerged tree the ground hardened and I staggered slowly up a heavy bank of less waterlogged peat to gain a hillock of heather and gorse. It was time to sit and let the water run out of my clothes while I considered how long it was between nightfall and dawn. I could see nothing now, even if I had had the inclination to shoot, which I had not. What about home ? Would they be sending out searchers for me now? Would they consider that I had headed this way in the first place because the duck had been in the lying corn the binder hadn't lifted, and would anyone believe that I could have been so reckless as to risk my life for three mallard? I didn't like to think what would be said or what reply I could make. I squelched my feet in my water-filled boots and idly thought again about the moment when I had stood dry on firm ground with the mallard coming fast right at me. I had to smile in spite of everything. It was a timeless, everlasting pleasure, a hunter's pleasure, a marksman's delight, something ancient that only my kind could appreciate. Wet and wretched as I was, I knew it couldn't be made into any sort of equation; and that second high shot, hadn't that been the essence of co-ordination of hand and eye used against the incredible ability of a duck that could sweep over a marsh and climb into the sky in seconds?

Inevitably waiting for the flight becomes a sort of compulsion stimulated by images and dreams. As the dedicated fisherman's mind may become obsessed with thoughts of fish rising in clear, remote waters, the mind of the embryo fowler is continually conjuring pictures of duck skimming along the river, planing in with tails down and heads set forward to alight, or of lesser members of the duck tribe, waves of wigeon at flight, or teal flashing across the water meadow and showing that they are the neatest fliers of them all. Eternally there is the artist's picture of black duck against the pale moonlit sky, echelons of them passing on their secret journeys in the night. Between the dream and reality there is many an unkind awakening. The wind of the morning whispers in the reeds, takes the last dead leaves away across the bleak meadow – and gnaws at the exposed cheeks, the nose, the uncovered fingers. When it comes from the east the dawn isn't an artist's dawn at all, but a Siberian grey that makes everything look as bleak as the far edge of the world. This wind takes the very air out of a man's lungs and he steps from one foot to the other, his blood no longer warmed by excitement and anticipation.

It doesn't always follow that duck, moving at last from their far-out rafting place, follow the well-known route by sandbank, runnel and feeder to the fowler's stand. The prevailing wind may veer or back and there they go, a hundred yards off course, oblivious to the danger they have escaped, dropping down in hurried squadrons to flap and preen and explore. The fowler watches with the same frustration as the fox that surveys the breeding pens or the hen-run with its high netting. This is the test that the enthusiast must pass again and again, season after season, until he is old and his blood can no longer withstand the frozen air of the morning, the bite of the wind at nightfall when it drives the duck upriver to feed. It is the test that makes the fanatic and sheds the dabbler, the dilettante and the mere amateur who seeks the glamour without understanding the nature of fowling.

Wild duck, like many other things, are where they are found. They vary in the sort of places they frequent, and they vary in edibility according to feeding. When the inland feeding grounds are frozen hard and they move out towards the seaboard and the muds, they have the flavour of the mud and sometimes a fishiness that requires some skill on the cook's part, but then a muddy pike presents the same problem, and the fowler who brings back a moorhen needs to advise the kitchen how to make it presentable. The duck that feeds on the stubble, and the barley stubble at that, is perhaps the best of all. To discover the feeding place of duck while there is still a field of late-lying corn is like finding gold and to stand and wait for the flight when the twilight lingers and the half moon slowly climbs has its special magic. People who know their duck and study the crops mark down the barley fields and the places they have noted of old as being the favourite places for flighting birds.

Nothing lasts or lingers for long when seasons wear and give place to one another. It is no use going to the oak and the beech when the tree is bare, for the pigeon will have discovered that it couldn't fill its crop and have sought some new source of food. The stubbles bleach and go back to the earth all too soon and the duck quickly alter their feeding pattern when they find that the pickings have become poor. I was fortunate in having access to places where all sorts of water-birds flighted, water-meadows that were private, a bog that was preserved, or the estuary which was free. I could stand where I liked in acres of stubble or on the fringe of growing corn that might not be cut until late September. The old man when he grew barley had always made arrangements with the distillery. It was a bespoke crop destined for the mash vat.

When a fine rain came in the afternoon and the sky was overcast the duck could come from a dozen different places. They were plump and in first-class condition and if one had patience great sport was to be had. Many a time I waded the corn to pick up my birds and came home as wet through as I should have been had I waded the river. I thought nothing of it any more than I did of standing in a loch on a November day, the cold water lapping at my thighs.

The older a wildfowler gets the more he studies how to make himself comfortable. Like the old soldier he begins to realise that morale depends on personal comfort. If he continually gets as wet as the store cattle grazing the grass banks of the estuary, lacking their thick hide and water-shedding coat of hair, he will shortly find that the twinges in his shoulder prevent him swinging his gun. He will sit at home and debate whether he should go out in the early morning or in the late afternoon on a winter's day. He will be old and have only wearisome tales to tell. There are all sorts of comforters that deal with the cold and not a few enthusiastic fowlers carry flasks to counteract the wind of the morning, sacrificing their reflex for inner warmth. The beginner may take heed of the cold both by carrying a flask and clothing himself in everything he can get under a duffel-coat and over a string vest.

Flighting is often a most static business, a position once taken having to be maintained come hell or high water. The difficulty with heavy layers of clothing is that they tend to tire even a strong man. They restrict movement and affect the gun mounting and altogether achieve no more, and in fact often a lot less, in the way of insulation than light clothing permitting free movement. The disturbing truth is discovered when the beginner tumbles into the creek wearing his heavy covering. It becomes ten times heavier when it is wet. Even if the duffel-coat has only been soaked with rain it is a great load to carry across a desert of mud that holds the boots and tries to bring the traveller to his knees. Even away from the windswept estuary the homing fowler may discover that quite small quagmires are best not judged merely by their diameter!

I remember an occasion when, returning from a long expedition that followed the course of a moorland stream, I decided to short-cut the route home. On the way I crossed a ridge that led to a long slope on which here and there patches of water and round rushes were to be seen. Far ahead of me I could see that mallard were still hanging about these places and I hurried my steps to come up with them. I had almost broken into a run – my strides were more than a yard in length – when all at once I floundered and watched a mallard drake taking off like a calendar duck, his outspread wings a picture of blue and white, the brand on his neck showing, his head as green as the weed in the waterholes. I wallowed like a stricken beast. My gun and one arm slipped into the peat and I threshed to get free. Fortunately I had touched only the edge of the bog hole and at length I got out looking like something moulded in black earth. They told me afterwards I had escaped from a hole that had taken a Clydesdale horse. It had no bottom and nothing ever got out! This, of course, was one of the local legends. The hole was there all right. No one had ever posted it or thought to run a bit of fencing round it. The black-faced sheep were too wary and wise in the ways of the moor to venture anywhere near the hole. Had I been wearing anything but the lightest of clothing I should have gone down to join the legendary horse.

Quite apart from their sporting qualities, the mallard is a species of duck that I find particularly fascinating. It will nest in the meadow, away in the moor, on a bank above a remote lake or in a pollard willow. It will boldly take its family a mile or two on the public highway to introduce them to water and better feeding and it will display extraordinary bravery when the brood is threatened. No one with any feeling for wildfowl would harass a mallard to discover her nest, but it requires only a reasonable period of careful watching with glasses to discover the duck going furtively back through the grass or the heather to sit again on her down-covered hatching of eggs. Predators are always at hand to rob the nesting duck – the stoat, the rat, the carrion crow, the fox, the polecat and sometimes even the old loose-toothed badger.

The mallard once she has begun to incubate tends to sit tight and rely upon her natural colouring. The less disturbance she makes the less likely is she to be found by the predators that hunt by scent. The less she moves the less chance there is of her being detected by the sharp-eyed birds. As soon as the ducklings are out of their shells and sufficiently strong to face the journey to the water she leads them away. Once on the water they are comparatively safe. At least the fox and the stoat know that they stand little chance of taking the ducklings there, although the great gull may try and the peregrine stoop from far aloft. Pike, of course, are notorious for picking off the mallard's train of ducklings and this is one of the saddest things that can be witnessed. On many occasions I have fished for pike in and out of season (on private waters) to save the breeding duck from extermination. I once stood by a keeper who became aboil with rage as he watched a mallard leading eight ducklings to a small island and gaining the shore with but one of her family. That same day I landed four pike of no more than four pounds a piece and three out of the four had dined on duckling.

On another occasion I was walking round a lake where I had been unsuccessfully trying to take trout when, in a little bay, I discovered a mallard floating with her head under water and her throat ripped. The thing puzzled me until I found a duckling among the stones and it seemed to me that whatever creature had killed the duck had taken the brood, leaving this solitary survivor. The problem was what to do with the little thing. It had passed the dappled stage and seemed to have a fair turn of speed when it ran through the adjoining round rushes, but I had no doubt that the dead duck would attract other predators and soon the duckling would be discovered and killed. We had some broody hens at home at that time and I decided to take the duckling with me and see if one of the hens might be persuaded to accept it. When I slipped the duckling in beside the hen she didn't seem to mind at all, but shortly afterwards, when the newcomer ventured out again, he disturbed his foster-mother and made her fluff up her hackles. I was about to discover that she mistook him for a rat. He ran almost as fast as a scurrying rat and before I could bring him back to the nest box the broody hen rushed past me and pecked him to death.

I began to see how futile it can be to attempt to adjust natural tragedies. We might have had a tame mallard in the fowl run. Many people have reared them and taken great pleasure in watching their daily flights. I have never been sure how long the mallard remains domesticated. It seems to me that the water meadows would hold an almost irresistible allure for them. What Khaki Campbell or Indian Runner wouldn't take off into the rain if it could, and what free-flying, handsome drake would ever think of returning to the pen once he had taken his bearings and discovered the hidden mysteries of a thousand pools and meandering streams, reedy lochs and weedy water-holes?

There are all sorts of aspects of flighting that make an addict of the novice: the opportunities that such a pastime provides for contemplation. To me the duck has one outstanding characteristic – its ability to circle the world. The duck that come skimming down to the loch or the stream may have arrived from the marshes of the Far East, the jheels of India, a hundred thousand water-holes, inland seas, lakes, rivers and ponds. Yesterday, perhaps they were in company in Scandinavia, a week ago who knows where they were? They drop out of the sky and paddle around and get their bearings, upend to feed, at home, here or in North America. Let the swallows and the lesser birds confine their journeys north and south, the wild duck knows no such restriction and ranges from Alaska to Siberia and from Siberia across all of the far north.

TALK OF GEESE

A BEGINNER may wait for migrating geese and strive to intercept them for a season or two before he succeeds and knows the weight of the bird in his hand. An experienced fowler may help him to overcome this initial frustration and in fact some sort of apprenticeship is inevitable. Wild geese are among the wariest birds that fly and late in the season they flight with fine judgment, it would seem, for the exact range of a gun. Not for nothing were geese chosen as the sentinels of ancient settlements and the wild goose is much more alert to danger than the domestic bird. It has to be so. They flight in hundreds and come flocking in to a pasture on the edge of the shore, but they usually come keeping a keen watch and once they have alighted there isn't a second when a sentry isn't on lookout.

This protective watch is an interesting thing about birds feeding in company. Very hungry birds, or birds of any sort newly arrived in a district, may be too ravenous to raise their heads for the first brief spell of feeding, but very soon it comes about that the lifting of heads becomes sporadic and finally almost a pattern, and responsibility for the safety of the flock is shared. No single bird takes it for granted that the rest are keeping watch for him because birds without the instinct to look out for themselves are eliminated automatically. By chance or natural design this preserves the flock.

When the uneasy goose suddenly becomes motionless, its very stillness seems to alert or make nervous one or two close at hand. Perhaps they watch the uneasy one, but the moment this bird can stand the tension no longer, the air is filled by the sound of flapping wings, the flock tears itself from the grass. There is nearly always a sound reason for the flight. The sentinel bird hardly ever makes a mistake and yet even with neighbours already slightly affected by this tension, if the watching bird relaxes, the flock seems to be soothed and feeds on contentedly.

The rising of a great flock of geese has something grand about it. There is no arrowing away as with startled duck, no panic flight. Geese have a slower, more powerful take-off. They beat their way up into the air and make a great display of grey and white, something to be remarked for miles around. The geese have come off the field down there by the tide. People who know the shore look about for the man crossing the pasture to examine his wintering cattle, or the two dogs chasing one another with the abandonment of their kind, and meanwhile the geese talk to one another, set up a babbling that is distinct from their casual

talk as they cross the very canopy of heaven on migration.

The cry of the migrating goose is one of the most haunting of sounds. As far as I am concerned it takes me back to my earliest days when my ear was better tuned to the song of the blackbird, the call of the curlew wailing above the moss, than it was to anything the schoolmaster hoped to impress upon me. Some people can trace their ancestry by the family tree or parish records and count five hundred years. A great-uncle once produced a family record that showed that my forebears had farmed and lived in a particular part of the country for almost five hundred years. Allowing for errors – and the blind eye – he may have been accurate to some extent, distorting the facts only to claim chieftainship or royal blood in every other generation, which is, after all, human! I have never bothered very much about who married whom or where the unions were recorded, but I am certain that my ancestors lived in the north, that the country was hard and bleak and the cry of the migrating goose was seared into their souls, for it is a sound that moves me and did so when I was no more than five years old. It conjures up a picture that no one gave me, something that must have been there when I was in my mother's womb.

To the people of the far north it is winter when the geese pass. There is something ominous in the sight of the first echelons and in the sound that heralds their coming. The tundra is being reclaimed by the cold hand of winter, the northern seas are boiling, putting salt into the gale, and the lashing rain that sweeps in soon carries sleet. In a matter of days desolation returns to the bogs and the plains where once the midges thronged. Hills and mountains, rocks and crags are glazed with snow like some vast piece of confectionery, and the geese have gone south just as the petrels move before the storm. The breeding grounds are on the brink of the endless night and only very special forms of life are equipped to survive there. As the migrants come south every goose on the farm pasture hears their crying and stops grazing the turf to call in reply. This, too, is one of the sad sounds of dying autumn. The fat Emden and the Toulouse would take to the air if they could, but, alas, they are no more equipped to join the flight than a portly stockbroker is equipped to hunt the mountain for his food.

The pathos in the exchanges is something never to be forgotten and it persists while the migrants are approaching, as they pass overhead and go on out of sight. In the last minutes the talk of the geese is a poignant, tragic conversation. It may take a little time, but the endless waves end, and somehow to me it always seemed that when this happened the sky took on a darker colouring, the sun lost its brilliance as the domestic geese fell silent again. Anyone who sees the passing of geese is stirred not simply by the trailing lines of birds crossing the heavens, taking their bearings and slowly altering their flight line, but by primitive and primeval instincts. No doubt something other than the calendar and the falling of the leaves or the breaking of the bud gives a similar stimulus to the peasant of France or Italy who looks on the vineyard or the olive grove and knows, perhaps by the sound of a seasonable wind or the behaviour of a bird, that the eternal cycle of change is taking place.

In the north the geese come, the snow bunting and lesser birds are remarked, the last leaves begin to shrivel and the wind takes them from the thorn. Where the geese settle the predatory gunners look at the mudflats, the winding course of the river that creeps away to blend with the sea and sky at a misty horizon that is indistinguishable. Across these plains of mud, up into the fields the geese will come as they have done since the day when man hunted in a skin and carried no more than a spear or a bow and arrow.

Today the goose shooter may arm himself with a pump gun, a magnum, a five-shot auto and cartridges of great striking power. I doubt whether he shoots as many geese as his predecessor who was armed with more primitive weapons. The age of mass production has put standard weapons into the hands of average performers, but it hasn't solved the elementary problem of getting within range of a goose. That, thank goodness, is still a matter of fieldcraft and individual ability. Five-shot guns or even far-reaching guns give the goose shooter not a great deal of advantage over the old-time fowler with his muzzle-loader. Some of the old muzzle-loaders, it was claimed, reached a long way farther than the 'new-fangled' breech-loaders and the advantage of a second barrel was only an advantage when the man holding the gun had not only the ability to make a right and left, or left and right as the need arose, but the luck to get two shots. Even so, some of the wily old hands who had their favourite 'hidey holes' would equip themselves with two primed muzzle-loaders and they could reload remarkably quickly if the flock of geese happened to be unwary enough to cross again.

The percussion cap was dying a natural death when I handled a gun for the first time. It is true that in the more old-fashioned catalogues black-powder guns, caps and shot were still offered for sale, but one got the impression that these catalogues were intended for the North-West Frontier, where tribesmen and old soldiers, destined never to be discharged, fondly imagined that nothing was changing and what was good enough for father couldn't be bettered.

A few muzzle-loaders were still about. The old fowlers swore by them. Sometimes, I fancy, they not only swore by them but they swore at them, for when they wanted to reach out at a far-off grey-lag they were inclined to pour powder the way they poured a tot of whisky on a cold night and in consequence the muzzle-loader bucked and bruised a cheek or suffered a shattered stock that had to be reinforced with windings of wire.

One of these venerable guns was in my grandfather's house when my mother first went to stay there. Mother was about as unlikely a sportswoman as could be encountered in a day's travel, but that, my aunt assured her, could easily be altered. Every self-respecting woman should be able to go out and shoot herself a pheasant or even a rabbit, and what mother needed was a little target practice with the old fowling piece. Mother in her innocence imagined that a gun was something that simply had to be held in the hands, the eyes were closed and one braced one's self for the shock, and the trigger was pulled. This she did, resting the heavy old goose gun on the drystone wall. When the gun boomed and the smoke rose Mother was seen to be lying on her back four or more feet from the place in which she had stood. She was badly bruised and swore that never would she try to shoot again – and she never did!

Some weeks after this my grandfather, who would have reassured her concerning the sporting life, took out the old gun, loaded and primed it and fired a charge of chopped nails at a tin can. The gun unfortunately burst, took a nice little nick of flesh from the old man's cheek and a sizeable part of the ball of his thumb from his right hand. No one ever shot a goose with it down on the muds after that. I was given the useless old lump of iron to carry about and learn the ways of conducting myself in the field, but I wasn't there when the accident happened. I didn't know that it had knocked my mother off her feet. When that happened my birth day was exactly three months off. The accident didn't affect me. I came crying into the world like any other child. My maternal grandfather gave me a sovereign and my father's father gave me, among other things, the relic of his goose-shooting days!

Great concern has been expressed at different times for the goose population and concern is understandable. If an increasing number of would-be fowlers succeed in shooting the geese they seek – and they naturally turn towards the professional and the man who knows the way of geese – it might be that certain species of geese would become so seriously depleted as to endanger their survival. The interests of conservationists, ornithologists and sportsmen have to be solved by some common denominator, and fortunately the fact is well-appreciated by each section. Most experienced fowlers are in no danger of making mistakes. They know their birds. They are prepared to impose restrictions on themselves in certain conditions. They know well enough that a balance is desirable, essential, and unless this generation faces up to such facts the next will suffer.

Beyond the realms of reason, however, are the unenlightened people (on both sides, perhaps) who know very little about wild life. Responsible wildfowlers are horrified and indignant when they discover evidence of indiscriminate shooting at protected birds. The shore cowboy, the gun-happy youth, who blithely takes to the marsh or the estuary and shoots everything that vaguely resembles a goose or duck, is nothing short of a criminal and he is hard to come up with or take in the act. To this sort of person a cormorant is some kind of goose and a merganser is also a goose, and where these unfortunate birds fall beyond the tide or among rocks it matters not at all, the sea will take them away or cover them with weed.

In the United States things are well regulated because large numbers of Wild Life Service Wardens are on hand to check licences and permits as well as bags, and no one may shoot simply because he holds a gun licence. It isn't practicable to organise fowling in this country in this way, but it seems to me that the day will come when something will have to be done to control the use of guns through membership of accredited clubs, perhaps under the central control of an organisation such as W.A.G.B.I. Goose shooting is a sport liable to be regarded as suspect so far as those who take part in it are concerned, unless some form of regulation is brought about. In the meantime, unfortunately, things go merrily on and the image of the true sportsman is too often besmirched by mud that doesn't rub off.

There is a lot to be said for the professional guide to the marshes. Canada and America have more than their share of professional guides, although there, I am inclined to think, the degree of spoon-feeding to businessmen intent on obtaining trophies or bag limits has resulted in a somewhat cynical attitude to the whole arrangement. In this country a number of well-known and highly respectable one-time professional wildfowlers, or very experienced amateur wildfowlers, have set up in business as wildfowling guides. We have yet to see advertisements guaranteeing bags as professionals do in America, but it seems to me that so long as these centres are properly run and wildfowling clubs are particular about the sort of people they admit, a lot could be done to isolate the cowboys, the offenders against both law and standards of sportsmanship. A bloody-minded outlook isn't something that can be easily eliminated. It is a problem for the sociologist. The vandal with the gun that commits his crime on the shore is exactly the same as the one who hangs about the cafes in the heart of the city, carrying a knuckle-duster or a piece of bicycle chain.

Unfortunately, many newspapermen and their editors don't know a responsible shooting man from a gangster any more than they would know the difference between a grey-lag and a parrot, and for the purpose of making headlines this gap in their knowledge hardly makes a whit of difference; a man who uses a gun is a 'sportsman' and whatever he does reflects on sportsmen in general, hence the public's impression that we shoot until we are knee-deep in dead birds and that worn-out piece of cynicism about it being a fine day for going out to kill while the sun shines.

Are we shooting geese simply for the thrill of killing? Does the salmon fisherman catch a salmon simply to use the priest? It is no easy business and the flesh of a wild goose is as worthy of any cook's ability as many other things that find their way to the table, and at least in this sphere there are no thrills at second-hand, no working off of hates and frustrations while someone else is pounded into insensibility, no hysterical shouting and emotional rioting, but the elemental things that have concerned the race since the beginning, the skill of the hunter and the cunning and craft of his quarry, long-conditioned to elude him and survive.

10

CLANTY MOSS

◇◇◇◇◇◇◇◇◇◇◇◇◇◇◇◇◇◇◇◇◇◇◇◇◇◇

I HAD shot grouse before I set foot on Clanty Moss with a gun under my arm. Every August when the shooting started on the surrounding moors, the grouse that were disturbed from the fringes of these places came to a boggy bit of ground that was the nearest thing to a peat moss we had. There they congregated among the heather and basked in the sun until the harvest fields were left to themselves. They knew the way things were as surely as if they had been crows, and immediately the coast was clear there they were, a mixture of black game and red, feeding on the stooks and among the stubbles. I knew they had lookouts and I always went back with great caution, working my way up the field from stook to stook until I could safely step out and take a shot or two. They were even more wary than they would have been on the moss because they were on strange ground. They rose fast and skimmed over the fence to be lost in the brown background. Sometimes they went right over the boggy ground and sailed across the far-off drystone wall. I often wondered if they went right on to the edge of the moors and Clanty Moss itself.

Clanty Moss was a place to dream of, a blue-misted horizon, a place of heat haze and the eternally singing grasshopper; and its fragrance was on the breeze from the west, a fragrance of peat, of meadowsweet and heather, of honeysuckle that grew on the boundary banks along with bilberry cropped short by black-faced sheep, all the wonderful scents and perfumes of the wilderness. Out there the light was brighter, the clouds finer and slowdrifting. It was always summer. This, of course, was the dream, the image I liked to conjure up when I thought about the Moss. It was often hazed in rain or mist and the cloud hung low and crawled slowly across it to the timber, the wall of spruce that hemmed it in on its northern side.

I had been to Clanty Moss scores of times before I ever went there to shoot. Going to the Moss was a summer ritual. There was work to be done there, at least for my elders who were concerned with preparing and laying in a winter's stock of peat. Coal was used for the kitchen fire, but only peat would do for the fire in the sitting-room and parlour. No one relaxed as he should with a coal fire burning in the grate. A peat fire, now, that was something fit for a man at his ease! Every summer a day or two was set aside for peat cutting and another for setting up the peat to let the wind get at it. The peat moss marched the Clanty Moss and when we went there I always contrived to wander away and cross the big ditch that divided the two. This was no easy feat.

The same ditch could have drowned a horse and its banks were treacherous, but once I had found a crossing place I could wander without fear of being recalled or overtaken.

Clanty Moss was big enough to hide me. It hid a lot of things, from the great packs of grouse that took refuge there in the middle of the shooting season because the Moss was hardly ever disturbed by shooting parties, to countless black-faced sheep, two or three old donkeys and a number of goats. The birds of the Moss were so numerous that I never managed to identify them all. The curlew and the snipe were abundant, so too were the moorland mallard. Hawks were there and kestrels as well as owls that ventured out from the spruce woods at dusk. The night jar called at twilight and the grouse themselves protested when they were disturbed by wandering sheep. On the old thorn trees the black game would congregate in the early season to have their conventions and mock battles.

I had noted all these things before I was given permission to shoot there. My grandfather was a close friend of the man who owned Clanty. The place took its name from a huddle of buildings that had been a moorland farm. In my time the buildings were crumbling. The timbers on which the slates had been nailed had sagged and the slates had shed to the foot of the walls. There was barely enough shelter for the donkeys when they took it into their heads to come to the nettle-grown steading. The dwelling-house was still occupied by an old shepherd and his wife. They had no family to keep them company, but they made up for this by keeping a great brood of cats, several dogs and a flock of hens that must have been a sore temptation for the moorland fox.

Sometimes the grouse came into the steading and fed where the hens scraped the winnowings of chaff (obtained from some more fertile place) that had been dumped for them. Often grouse perched on the walls that surrounded the court and took off only when someone strange arrived on the scene. The shepherd and his wife left them at peace. The old man had a gun, but would never have thought of using it except to scare a crow intent on picking at a sickly lamb. Grouse were the prerogative of the gentry and not to be shot for a shepherd's dinner, even if there was no one to prevent this being done.

The peacefulness of Clanty Moss was something that I can hardly describe. It was crossed by a moorland road that hardly ever saw more than one or two vehicles a day and those were horse-drawn carts or gigs. Rabbits, a large proportion of them black ones, bobbed about the road from one side to the other. The road belonged to the wild creatures and not to man at all. Walking along the soft springy grass beside the wheel tracks one could put up a grouse or encounter a fierce falcon perched on a silver birch. The road ran away into the far distance, straight and true, two stony tracks where the wheels ran, two strips of green and a central stony strip where the hooves of horses prevented the grass spreading. One could have camped on that road, sat down in the middle of the track, or stretched out and gone to sleep there without fear of being disturbed from morning until night unless a tinker's cart came rolling along to make a short-cut from one of the little villages beyond the skyline to another far out of sight on the other side of the spruce woods.

The grouse came to the road as they always do. They needed grit to digest their food. The few times they were shot was when poachers waited for them to come for grit. The road was watched by the keepers of adjoining moors, who knew well that if they marked the cross-roads after hearing a shot they stood a good chance of identifying or catching the culprits. Grouse, even the grouse that lived on Clanty Moss, were wary on open ground without cover at hand. Anyone walking up the grey road could count on seeing the grouse moving ahead, slipping away into the heather and showing themselves no more. Only a poacher prepared to lie up in an alder clump or a damp ditch could hope to shoot the birds on the road and not even then, unless he was very lucky, could he reckon on bagging more than one. Once a shot was fired the keepers were alerted and the whole of the moorland listened and watched.

Grouse nest early in the year. Young grouse are often drowned when peat holes and drains are flooded. The hen leads them on from one place to another. It is imperative that she does so because they are always in danger from predators, and food is nowhere plentiful. The tallest heather buds out of reach of chicks and by the end of July they must all be able to fend for themselves. The whole moor has a short summer, a short breeding season. On

the fringes it seems that the bracken is hardly up before it loses its bright green and begins to age. The heather may be slow to show colour, but in an incredibly short time it will lose its lustre, bleach and die. The adder sleeps only a few weeks on the mounds of fine grass. Summer is late and short. When the apples are ripening in lowland gardens and the damson is drooping with fruit-laden boughs, the moorland rowan's berries are already crimson and the leaves touched with rust.

Grouse and black game are subject to great fluctuations brought about by wet springs, hard winters, summers when growth was retarded by east winds, but they are native birds, they belong on the moor and have been there since time immemorial, at least in small numbers. Keepers who look after the moor know how important it is to burn the heather to a pattern and what devastation their stocks of grouse may suffer through disease or flood, but they also know that both red and black game are conditioned to survive and if the moor went back to the jungle, without a single hawk or harrier being discouraged, one or two moorbirds would still be there no matter what.

Clanty Moss was in no danger of becoming bare of game when I was told that I might shoot there. There were vast packs of grouse to be put up, a few hares, scores of rabbits and a variety of fowl. I could hardly wait to arm myself, harness the pony to the gig, and drive there.

I went for the first time on a late August morning when the whole world was bathed in sunshine. The moor was as fresh and alive as ever it had been in spring and when I took the trouble to keep the pony's hooves and the wheels on the right tracks of grass I came upon some form of wild life every few hundred yards. Is there anything more stimulating than to shoot over land that hasn't been shot over for a long time and contains a great variety of game? I had the elation I often feel when I put up my rod on a new piece of water, some likely-looking loch or stream in which I have never cast before.

'Tell the old shepherd the post will bring him a letter today or tomorrow,' I had been told. All would be well. I wouldn't shoot too many grouse because I wouldn't get much opportunity of a second shot until I had tramped a mile or so. It wasn't an easy place to shoot without help in the shape of flanking guns and at least one or two dogs, deep-chested sturdy dogs that would carry through overgrown heather and struggle up and down the peat banks. Almost as soon as I had unyoked the pony, the old shepherd was out to see me, rubbing his bristly chin and making it plain that I had disturbed his rest. He nodded when I told him my name and the family connection. He didn't know me, but that hardly mattered. He knew 'the grandfather of me' and 'the great-grandfather' and that was more important.

'There it is then,' he said, waving a hand at the Moss, 'and I leave you to it! I couldn't keep up with you if I came and what would I be doing coming with you anyway?'

A small company of grouse sailed over us and planed down into the heather a hundred yards away, but I hadn't put my gun together and there were plenty more out in the heather as the old man said. I knew that, but although grouse have a way of perching on heather mounds and cackling, they also have a way of melting away and giving no indication of their possible where-abouts until one has walked them up.

No one can seriously shoot grouse without organisation. Anything short of teamwork is pottering and wouldn't be allowed on a well-conducted moor, but Clanty Moss was the excep-tion. It wasn't shot because its owner wouldn't have it shot and wouldn't rent it to his neighbours, but now and again, when he remembered his youth and his days with the gun, he relented and allowed someone to walk his ground. I thanked him mentally as I clambered over the wall where the stones had been tumbled into the bracken beyond. Clegs buzzed me as I waded through into the peat moss and I killed one drinking blood from my neck.

Inevitably, in such a state of excitement and elation, I missed the first grouse that rose. I watched the close at hand red game going, picking up others as they sped away. I had disturbed Clanty Moss for the first time in many months. All around me on far-out peat banks and in depressions rabbits bobbed and cocked their ears and hares went hopping nervously out of sight along their secret paths to remote places. The black game and the red game stopped their basking on the flattened heather, their heads cocked, their senses alert, for some of them had come from the adjoining moors.

The black cock is a wily bird, but one not hard to pick out when he takes flight. He seems to rise with an awareness of his singularity, never rising first, but never being far from the heart of the pack, hugging the contours as he goes. I knew that before I had gone far I would flush him and when the moment came and the dense pack rose, there he was, travelling with the swing of my gun, tumbling as the shot took him, the white feathers, the brand on blue showing as he struck the heather. I had no head to take a second shot. I let the rest go and hurried to pick him up. As I went forward a straggler rose and my second shot doubled my kills.

I looked back at the stunted tree growing in the comer of the farm steading. It seemed miles away and hours away in time. The heat made it more indistinct, like an out-of-focus photograph. Somewhere in one of the depressions of the Moss a donkey brayed and a cock grouse flew up and alighted again, complaining after the manner of his kind, disturbed a second time. The thirty or forty birds I had put up had been swallowed by the heather except for that one vociferous bird and he was half a mile from me down and across the old peat cuttings. I found myself thinking that there was something about all this that reminded me of fishing the moorland stream, the calling grouse was like a fine brown trout rising in a lonely pool, turning at the fly and going deep into the shelter of the peat bank to rise again some other time.

I suppose that if I hadn't shot a hare towards the end of the afternoon, when my shirt was sticking to my back and my thigh muscles were beginning to ache, I might have finished with three brace of grouse or even more, but I was tested by the hare, a hare I could have shot on one of our own hills or in the bog. It ran round me in a circle as I turned. When I fired I discovered that I had somehow walked into another great pack of grouse, but I was off balance, my foot slipping on the bank as they took wing and my shot went through a hole in the flight! They went away like hedge-hopping aircraft. I watched them until I lost them in the background and didn't know where they alighted. There had been four or five lyre-tailed cocks among them, but I had my birds and it was no longer a matter of urgency to come up with them. One man can't hunt a moor and make much of an impression on moor fowl.

The old shepherd had come out to the well to watch me coming back. He saw the odd bird rising ahead of me and to be fair to him he shouted and waved in the hope of turning them back to me, but nothing he could do could persuade them to turn about. They had all the moor on either side, as far as the eye could see. I took my time coming down. I was content as I was when I had been all day walking the bank of the stream. The Moss had intoxicated me, soothing and tiring me at the same time. Whatever fire I had had was spent. I breathed the peat smoke from the farmhouse chimney, looked at the distant hills beyond the farmland and the bay while the moor settled again, the black-faced sheep bleated and the donkey brayed.

'You got one of them old black cocks then,' the shepherd said. 'They tell me you might as well eat a ball of string soaked in gravy.'

'We'll hang him,' I promised.

'You'll have to do that. When the maggots have had their fill you'll have yours.'

There didn't seem much point in offering the old fellow a moor bird. Whether he had eaten his fill of them or not he seemed to have a low opinion of black cock.

'It was hardly worth the walk,' he commented, 'but maybe you saw an old black-faced tup up there, one with a broken horn?'

I was sorry to say I hadn't because he had given me a sense of guilt at passing the whole day in such a feckless manner. He struck at a stone with the end of his long crook and went limping over the gap in the wall, telling me without words what he thought about people who went out on the Moss to shoot, but his wife accepted the hare. If they didn't have it with potatoes it would do for the cats she said. She would not have a moorbird. If anyone came and found the feathers or the bones they would think that her husband was a poacher and he wasn't. Besides, they were tough, strong-tasting brutes and only fit for the gentry who overcame the taste with lashings of wine.

The pony tossed his head and let me put the collar on. He was ready for the road. The clegs had been bothering him and he was weary of the sight of the wall. The oats were all gone. I had to hold him in to ensure that we went home at a leisurely pace in keeping with my mood, disturbing nothing but the rabbits that hopped away when we were almost on top of them.

Subsequent visits to Clanty were in the same sort of pattern. I recall them now when I look at the high white clouds of summer, when I see the blue mist on the hills and smell peat burning. Nostalgia is a strange thing, a separate compartment of the mind in which yesterday is kept bright and clear, requiring only some small thing to unlock it all. I find it happens when I handle a certain old hammer gun, when I look down at the fine grass of the moor and see the curling shoots of young bracken coming through, when the curlew cries — wherever I happen to be — when a long twisting line of smoke tells me that the hill shepherds over there on the mountain are burning the old growth to provide potash for next year's pasture.

The old shepherd has long since gone the way of all good shepherds and Clanty Moss has changed. The timbers of the slate roofs have slumped more and more and the slates have shattered. I passed the place only last summer, this time going slowly in a car but losing the atmosphere. The key didn't open the door. There were no rabbits bobbing on the turf at the road verge. The road itself was tar-patched and had lost its endless green ribbons of grass. No grouse cackled. I didn't see either red or black game along the whole length of the Moss and when I reached the cross-road and the moor village they told me that grouse were as rare as the corncrake.

Something had happened to reduce the stock beyond the point of recovery. Perhaps the war had contributed something. It could have been that vermin had multiplied, and that one season after another flood and natural disaster had banished the black cock from a place where it had seemed to me they had lived and bred since the beginning of time.

Is there some great difference in the present decade? One could hardly argue that the difference is significant because there are still grouse moors well-stocked with grouse, and keepers to look after them, but there are fewer grouse moors and fewer keepers, more forestry tracts and cover for vermin, and if this in itself isn't very significant, perhaps the really significant thing is

that nowhere is remote any more and what we take for peacefulness isn't to be compared with the holy silence of moors and the
wild country forty or fifty years ago.

ROUGH SHOOTING
IN THE HILLS

◇◇◇◇◇◇◇◇◇◇◇◇◇◇◇◇◇◇◇◇◇◇◇◇◇◇

IN the course of something like twenty years in Wales I have shot over all sorts of ground and most of it wild and unkeepered ground at that. Making friends among the farmers is something that comes instinctively to me, for my father's family had only an odd blacksmith and weaver among them, apart from farmers, over something like five hundred years, if I take the only document I have inherited as being reliable and authentic. Getting permission to shoot and extending the territory as acquaintanceships ripened took me farther and farther afield and perhaps the only drawback in the end was the difficulty in keeping up the rounds and covering the territory often enough to maintain contact. I was as ready for the field as the most eager newcomer when I began, but time has slowed me a little and now I sadly remember shooting I once enjoyed, without having to do more than call and say I was on my way round. In some places I took tea and was expected to call and sit for a while. In others they waved me cheerfully on and I lost no time in going through the copse or walking the rough. I knew places where the buzzards nested and the peregrine hunted, places where the duck came down to little isolated pools and streams that over-flowed their banks, corners where an old cock pheasant regularly hid himself and his wives kept him company.

I shot the crow and the stoat, the magpie and the jay. I was my own keeper of the game and knew every secret the ground held. This freedom was the sort I had enjoyed as a youngster. How long it might have lasted I don't know. I had a number of distractions. There were occasions when I concentrated on shooting woodpigeons in particular woods, a while when I joined forces with another wandering gun and we went to the river to see what we could do with duck below the tideline and the limit of the salt.

I used to shoot at Ty Newydd once a week. It had two small woods, a hazel copse and a winding stream that ran down through the centre of the farm. It was on Ty Newydd that I saw my last corncrake in Wales. It rose on a gorse slope at the tail of a hilly bit of ground where they had been cutting hay and it went clumsily round me, making me turn on my heel to see what it was. I had come up at the request of the farmer to shoot pigeons that were on a field of peas and corn. I told him about it and it was he who suggested that the corncrakes hadn't gone at all but had fallen silent, a delightful little fairy story thought up by a man whose father had been a bard and won awards at the Eisteddfod. It was on Ty Newydd, too, that I saw a second hare rise where a dog ran one into cover and was misled by the fresh runner, proving it to myself by going down and flushing the one I had first seen.

Rabbits were abundant at that time and I was expected to make frequent visits to keep them down. They were reproachful when I failed to turn up.

'We cut the hay on the top,' they would say. 'The rabbits were worse than fleas on a hedgehog and where were you? You didn't come! You'll have to knock some over or we'll have to get a chap to snare them.'

They had no intention of doing any such thing. I had become an event in their week. I stopped to talk when they were sorting the potatoes and they told me where the partridges had gone. I crossed to pass the time of day with the old fellow at the clamps and he warned me to go carefully down through the gorse. Three pheasants had been on the bank that very morning and if I had no luck there I should go up to the water-hole on the way to the long fir plantation. Two duck had flown round it several times during the week.

An intimacy with the ground as well as with the people who live and work on it is an essential thing to be developed by a casual shooter. There is more to knowing the land than simply having looked at it from a distance or walked through it once or twice. Fields and woods change from one day to the next, as the wind blows, the sun shines or the driving rain passes over or through them, and the man who is always on the ground, like the man who lives on the bank of a river, has great advantages. Which way will the old cock pheasant run to break cover and where and how will he rise? Exactly where does he sit and how long will he stay hidden? These are questions the native doesn't have to ask. He knows, and knows precisely, what the ground will produce because he has lived on it, because he has

seen everything over and over again. He can't be surprised, nor does he suffer from the tension of anticipation in places where nothing happens.

It is a fact that some sort of extra-sensory perception guides the hunter, but a feeling for the ground depends on his absorbing the atmosphere first. Let him walk a wood once or twice, kick through the bracken, follow a stream and he knows that these are more than likely places. They are the haunts of game. I have always considered that I have been blessed with this sort of gift. Even more than when I am abroad with the gun I am aware of it when I stand by the water with a rod in my hand. This is not to say that I catch more fish than the next man or anyone else with the same degree of skill, but I know when I am going to catch fish. I know that the fish are there and often I know precisely when a rise is going to come even after an hour or two without a single indication of the presence of a fish. In the field one may be surprised by the sudden flight of a woodcock or a snipe or be misled into thinking that there is nothing to be put up, but concentration produces a negative or positive answer and hundreds of times I have had my instinct confirmed.

In places well-stocked with game of different sorts this sense is hard to demonstrate. It has always been on rough ground that I have found it operative. I have walked a field that was apparently bare and known that in the corner, materialising from the ground itself, I would put up a hare. It might be said that a likely field for a hare prompts the intuition and that when the hare rises one remembers that the guess was right. When nothing happens the whole thing tends to be forgotten. There is no reason to remember failure. This may be so. Everyone must have a theory of one sort or another to explain anything that isn't a matter of simple arithmetic and in fact can't be added up.

I know water that holds fish. Unlike some people, I have never fished in lakes ruined by lead or copper washings. I catch fish where I know there are fish. I don't need to be told that the fish are there, and the place for a hare, a covey of partridges, a solitary mallard or a wild cock pheasant, acts upon me as I imagine a hazel rod does upon the water diviner. Laugh if you like, but I am sure that it is an inheritance from my ancestors and I am sure that I am not the only hunter or angler who is aware of such things. They tell me that I am a lucky man with a gun and a fly rod. No one has ever remarked that I possess a particularly great skill. I am ready and willing to admit that I am average or even below average, but the field and the river have a message for me and it has nothing to do with the ordinary senses. My eyesight is good, my hearing fair. There was a witch in the family once and this is something I would not joke about!

I used to shoot in company with three other enthusiasts who were prepared to tramp as much as twenty-five miles in a day. They were a light-hearted set of companions, always cheerful and ready to plod on. Two of them were highly competent shots given to experimenting with guns, cartridges, loads, etc. and the third something of an expert with dogs. One of the stretches of ground across which we shot was a wilderness grown up after a sizeable wood had been felled for logs and here we often found ourselves tested by rabbits dashing from one bit of undergrowth to another, by woodcock that rose from sections of boggy ground and rotting leaves, by an odd hare or two, a pigeon that dallied in an ivied stump the fellers had disdained to bring down, and companies of wild pheasants that remained until the last minute before exploding all round us. It depended how tired we were and how good our co-ordination was what sort of bag we made. The black labrador generally confirmed or denied our claims to having killed something that fell out of sight. The shooting was fast but often sporadic and there could hardly have been better snap-shooting.

I remember one day being persuaded to try some brass cartridges one of the party had been at pains to recap and load. Perhaps the light had been against us or it may have been that the sort of shots that had presented themselves were beyond even the best of us, but at the end of the day we had a pitifully small bag to show and I couldn't refrain from suggesting that the cartridges weren't what they might have been. It might be old advice to say never look a gift horse in the mouth, but I was inclined to think that the charge was wrong or the shot wasn't shot at all but rock salt which my grandfather had recommended for shooting turkey thieves at Christmas time!

The member of the party responsible hotly defended his ammunition and his loading machine and I scornfully suggested that even at less than twenty-five yards he wouldn't be able to make the slightest impression on my old hat, a hat I may say, I was fond of and wouldn't have risked had I not been convinced that I was right. To prove my point I tossed the hat in the air and my three companions fired at it. It fell absolutely undamaged. 'There,' I said, 'will you believe me now? You loaded these brass cartridges with dust!' I stepped back a couple of yards and took careful aim at my hat and pulled the trigger and my much loved hat disintegrated! My companions almost died of laughing at the expression on my face. Two of them had held off my hat. The cartridge-loader had missed and I had wrecked my hat. No one suggested that I should follow this by eating it!

Such irresponsibility wasn't characteristic of our outings, I hasten to add. It isn't by chance that I recall the incident and have forgotten most of the bags we made and the difficult shots my companions demonstrated. It brings happiness to recall our laughing in the late October sunlight and my ruefully putting a hand through the shattered hat and admitting that somehow some lead had got into one of those brass cartridges! I have always been a sentimentalist about old coats and old hats and association has been the means of many pleasant recollections.

I was shooting at Ty Mawr when I slipped and damaged the old Damascus barrelled gun and when I chance to handle it now I think of the blustery wet afternoons when I came back to the farmyard with my coupled rabbits and the odd bird, the shaggy Welsh collies sniffing at my bag and back-trailing to find where I had paunched the rabbits behind the drystone wall. It was on the way to this farm that we passed through another farm court in which a mangy collie was chained in a hole with only a slate covering over him. The man who considered this a kennel was one of the most uncouth characters I have ever encountered – the sort of barbarian who would strap up a dog's leg in the early stages of its training and keep it strapped until it shortened, making a wayward dog biddable.

At Ty Mawr one stepped out of the century into the farm of the nineteenth or even the eighteenth century. The place was furnished with the traditional Welsh dresser, those ancient, rickety spindle-backed chairs, the inevitable oak settle, brass candlesticks and the swinging lamp, the bread crock and the buttermilk jug. We wouldn't be able to leave without tea and stone-baked scones, red gooseberry jam to follow cheese, and the butter was pot butter with a slightly cheesy flavour. Our clothes steamed and we ate ravenously as we talked about the woodcock we put up or how we had snapped at a rabbit heading for the stream and watched it carried down in the flood, disappearing under a half submerged log. The old man was something of a shot himself. His eye was better than his eyesight, one might say. He shot well by instinct and he took a pride in seeing a good bag whether he had contributed a gun or not.

'You could have done better if you had come Tuesday,' he would say. 'The rabbits was lying out then, hundreds of them and there was red grouse down off the moor. Three or four I seen when I was up at the sheep in the top field.'

The rent wasn't much for a rough shoot and I was only a visitor, but it amused me when the old fellow went out of the way to shoot over his own ground and bring the pheasant he obtained to his tenant demanding – and receiving – the current market price for it! On occasions it was quite plain that the place was being heavily shot between our visits. Could we protest when the old fellow, knowing that we might spot the rabbit fur here and there on the open field, informed us that our trouble was that we weren't shooting often enough to keep down the rabbits and he was having to take care of the vermin in both his own and our interests? The situation eventually led to the shoot being given up. It was a hopeless proposition and should never have been accepted in the first place, but, suffering no personal loss, I still cherish those visits to Ty Mawr and the tea we took by candle-light on wild evenings when the light had gone and we came in from the hill.

Rough shoots are like gold in the Welsh hills. Most of the easily acquired places are vermin-ridden and barren of game. Hill partridges know nothing of march walls or boundaries. The hare, too, is often confused as to his proper place and without the rabbit many of the places agents are pleased to call shoots deserve the name only because at times game strays from estates that are heavily shot during the early days of the season.

To cultivate a shoot in rough country, largely consisting of scrub and harbouring alarming numbers of predatory creatures, is, like pioneering on the North-West Frontier, carving something out of the wilderness. Few people have the heart for such long-term investment and even finding a place worthy of the effort and with the makings of a shoot is far from easy. Too many novices with money to spend push up the price of indifferent ground and too many agents who don't know a pheasant's tail from its elbow advertise shooting that really isn't shooting at all, but a sort of providential, migratory stock of birds of one sort or another.

There may be Crown Land shooting advertised under tender once in so many years, but this is territory that is gathered in by the sort of syndicate that covers as much ground as it can rent and trusts to luck. It takes a long time to come upon a place that lends itself to preserving, that can be watched and tended, cultivated and cleared at the same time, and there is always the problem of finding a trustworthy warden to keep off the local poachers.

The size of a manageable rough shoot depends on the terrain and its boundaries and when these are limited there is always the final limitation of the number of guns the place can accommodate and the number of days in the season that shooting may reasonably take place. It is an easy enough matter to find partners in a shooting enterprise. Enthusiasm is infectious and there is always the novelty of the unknown ground. Some friends of mine let themselves be carried away to the extent of stocking a newly-acquired shoot and then were dismayed to find that their freshly-released poults had a gipsy characteristic or behaved like rainbow trout and melted away before they could be taken again.

Old keepers know what happens when birds are released too soon for a special occasion. Having no roots in the place, and being unfamiliar with the ground, the strangers are likely to wander aimlessly on and on, as stupid as battery birds pitched out on to the open field. Being unaware of the natural shelter the newcomers must move and watch out for the hawk or the fox. When they take flight they have all the points of the compass from which to choose and even if the shoot happened to be signposted it is doubtful whether the birds could read!

The bird that thrives is the wild bird. It is checked by the number of predators that frequent the ground. It can be fostered by the destruction of these vermin and provided all the things game need are present it may multiply, but a handful of seed needs a considerable amount of attention if there is to be a natural return and the same applies to building a stock on a rough shoot. Too much cover may harbour too many predators and too drastic cutting back can expose the small stock of game.

As with farming, the man who tends his acres may expect to take out in ratio to what he puts in and his experience will have to be bought, as my friends found out when their investment failed completely and they bagged only one of several dozen birds they so hopefully released.

Stocking and hand-rearing are matters for the expert in the management of game. Every old keeper has his own secret preparation for keeping his birds at home and knows just how many hours of daylight he must invest to earn congratulations after the first big day of the season. Far removed from this specialist field is the owner of the little rough shoot. His investment may not be in hours spent on the rearing field and watching out for the hawk, but it will certainly mean shooting or trapping many head of vermin for every brace of pheasants he brings back, and haunting his ground while the birds breed and grow in order to discourage every kind of raider from the two-legged vandal to the hunting cat.

Incidentally, it has seemed to me of recent years that the domestic cat turned wild is increasing in numbers. I have wondered whether this may or may not have something to do with the great improvement in methods of exterminating rats and mice including certain poisons. There was a time when the farm cat was allowed the run of the place and was fed saucers of milk ad lib. The cat did invaluable service in killing the rats that infested the hen-run and the rick butts. Today the cat is begrudged his milk. He is a pest. There are fewer keepers to control the now feral cat and it winds its way through wood and copse and undergrowth every bit as big a menace as the stoat. I am often awake early and, looking out of my window, I have counted three or four apparently wild cats hunting our woods day after day. A time may come when the cat surpasses the stoat and weasel tribe completely and takes as big a toll of young birds – partridges, pheasants and the like – as crows, jays, magpies and all the rest put together.

It is illegal to set traps in the open and the law forbids poison. It seems to me that the cat has everything in his favour! We are grateful for the pheasants that stray on to our ground from the adjoining estate and shoot them in season without compunction, our excuse being that we are stopping them from straying farther out, but how many birds are hunted out of our territory by domestic cats gone wild it grieves me to think, and how many more birds our neighbour would have if the cats were destroyed I can't imagine.

At the moment of writing I am without a shoot of any sort and my thoughts are of wildfowling and occasional day's pigeon shooting, but a friend is pressing me to turn again to a rough shoot in some unspecified corner of wild Wales, a bit of marshland, an acre or two of peat, a few more of scrub trees and quite a stretch of grazing. This is the old eldorado of dreams where the mallard flight, the hare sits up, the cock pheasant runs through the bracken, teal spring from the pool, God's in His heaven and all's right with the world. In spite of my grey hairs I find myself inclined to fall for it again, banishing the thought that there is no such thing as something for nothing!

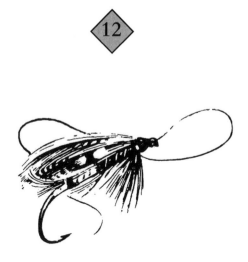

ABOUT WITH A ROD

◇◇

LARGE numbers of shooting men wind up with a rod in their hands when the season is over. Some take to fishing to fill in the time and never seriously get the bug. Some seek the things they most enjoy in the field and wood, the sheer delight of the open air. Most are biased in favour of shooting rather than fishing. A fanatical fishing enthusiast thinks about nothing else even during the close season and some shooting enthusiasts fish with a preoccupation they can hardly disguise. Their conversation drifts from what is happening in a particular pool right up through the water-meadows to the comings and goings of the nesting mallard and to the cocks that venture down from the woods. A fish rises and they miss it. They curse and bring their mind back to the task in hand. If the sea-trout are up it won't be too long before grouse and duck are in season. By the time the autumn run is on the partridges will be full-grown and the longtails running the woods as thick as sparrows at the threshing.

I have always found that the river and the stream held as much of a magnetic attraction as the marsh or the moor, but then I was probably subjected to disturbing influences and lack of strict guidance when I was a small boy. One urged me to snare a rabbit and another would make a fisherman of me, show me how to take an eel, point out the 'hidey hole' of a good trout, talk a lot of intriguing stuff about the size of a big ged (pike). Some geds could take a horse by the nose, snap up a falling duck or come from the depths with a ferocity and force that would send spray high into the sunlight as they seized prey not just on the water, but from the air above it, a flighting swallow for instance!

Now some people take to fishing late in life. They are often rather fumbling fishermen, but they generally turn out to have been pretty successful businessmen and to have concentrated on the really important job of gathering money to enable them to enjoy their leisure. They are single-minded and in the end they make a fair fist of the new sport. They buy the best tackle and they fish in the right places, which is more than half the battle. The lifelong fisherman somehow turns out to be a sort of misguided soul who could never for long enough put away his toys and his playthings or take his mind from day-dreaming in order to become rich – to have his cake and eat it.

Who would you be if you weren't you? The question baffles this fellow. He can't think whom. There just wasn't enough time available for the business of being who he was. Ask him where he would have fished if he could have chosen and the answer is there – in Ireland, Scotland, Norway, Canada, New Zealand, in places where the marlin swims and the dolphin pilots the craft, in the High Sierras, the Andes or in turbulent, mysterious waters where the mahseer is to be taken. There is something about this fellow that makes him seem a little out of this world. Can fishing be so important to anyone that he simply lives and breathes it? I have never been able to say how bad my bug is, but I had a pretty serious case when I was small. I think it was rather like cow-pox, which I had so badly that the doctors said I would never contract smallpox! I look at every piece of water I pass and wonder how unpolluted it is, what weeds may grow in it, would it support a good trout, a fat tench, a long-snouted old pike, a school of rudd or a plump perch?

The water in which I fished mainly contained trout. I didn't need to go far to find a perch or a pike. Eels were plentiful everywhere. The rivers were salmon rivers that came up when it rained. Salmon fishermen seemed to emerge in the rain on even the loneliest country roads. One encountered them at any time of the day, plodding along in their waders and oilskins with enormous, already-assembled salmon rods in their hands and gaffs dangling from their belts. They fished the fly, the worm and various baits. Some of them used spinning tackle, but spinning hadn't really come into its own. The threadline reel was in its teething stage and not only that, it was expensive. The elite, the skilled, the knowledgeable fished the fly and took their fish on it when the water was in order. Today a large number of anglers carry the flyrod for appearance's sake, it seems to me, and fish the shrimp. But a good few of these old experts didn't even go to the river until it was in condition for the fly.

My first serious expedition with a salmon rod and a fly had a humiliating result. The water was in condition. There was no doubting that. I was told when and where to go. I could fish a fly for trout by that time, but for some reason the salmon passed me and three times I hooked, played and landed fish of three to four pounds – pike that took the Silver Doctor or whatever it was

I had on! I killed my pike and said nothing about them on my return. I had already found that sometimes a good trout taking the wet fly turned out to be a greedy perch.

It was some years before I graduated to dry-fly fishing. The dry-fly has the merit of letting the angler see what is happening and the additional advantage of ensuring that the fish, nine times out of ten, is hooked well and truly, driving the barb home by the violence of his turning. All the mystery of nymph fishing, the intriguing business of deep-working, large lake flies must be put aside in order to enjoy the sheer delight – less frequently enjoyed than the taking of fish by other methods – that goes with dropping the fly on the expanding rings made by a rising fish. There is nothing in this world, so far as I am concerned, that comes within the same transport of the spirit, the sheer, heart-beat-suspending ecstasy that this moment promotes; nothing else, anywhere or in any circumstances, within the realms of such rapture.

No one introduced me to dry-fly fishing. I fumbled my way into it, fishing in difficult waters for more-than-difficult fish. I cast in so many places that were next to impossible to reach that I acquired a certain ability to put a fly where I wanted it or to make it end up where the fish had risen. My technique would probably raise smiles among the chalk-stream experts. I fish too hard, too keenly, I think, for fish that are well-provided with food on streams where the mayfly is found, fly-boards are installed, or liver supplied to encourage lusty fish. I should, I confess, be a little ashamed to demonstrate the way I fish for fear that they might think I also shot pigeons round the dovecote!

To fool a small trout is not difficult. Small trout are eager and unconditioned in their way. They feed eagerly and without much discrimination because they must feed. If they have anything to teach it is in the speed with which they must be struck if one is fishing the wet-fly, or the changes that must be rung if the dry-fly is missed, because, although they will come again, they come best at a new pattern. I began dry-fly fishing on turbulent waters, fishing under over-hanging trees and in rocky pools. I graduated to lakes because I fell for the mystery of these places. A large number of mountain lakes that contain fair trout have a very poor and brief hatch of flies. The fish are largely bottom-feeders and take mostly beetles and crustaceans for the greater part of their feeding cycle. There are days when the large lake olive sails on the surface, when little dimples denote the hatching nymph and the rings of feeding trout mark the change to surface feeding. To be perfectly truthful, I never found that colour or exact imitation of the fly mattered to any appreciable degree. Size and surface pattern – that is, the impression of legs or the 'buzz' of wings above the skin of the water – are vital. All the dyeing of plumes and the selection of herl, silk and so on seems to me to be removed from reality and belong primarily to the art of making artificial flies which in turn is as far removed from fishing as the building of an igloo is from constructing a penthouse.

The two most important things in fly-fishing, in my opinion, are in the presentation of the fly and the avoidance of the skyline – that is, being sure of the camouflage of one's background. Trout may be disturbed by the shadow of a heavy nylon cast lying across the stones or a hook like a ship's anchor penetrating the surface skin because of the lack of supporting hackles. To this degree the selection of terminal tackle is important, but who can prove that a fish has a micrometer built into its eye, an optical measuring device that records the difference between ·003 in. and ·004 in. when a human hair may be no more than ·002 in.? Perhaps I was fortunate in coming to dry-fly fishing without the guidance of those who dabble with it. I discovered that a No. 18 or 20 hook and a cast of ·003 in. isn't exactly the thing for a lusty lake trout. It needs something with more iron to penetrate the hard jaw of a large lake trout, toughened by bottom feeding most of the season. It certainly needs stronger stuff to hold him than ·003 in. nylon. It is true that many experts fish with no more, but they don't fish in rocky lakes where they must cast to and hook a fish that shows perhaps once in a day and maybe only once in a week of days!

Long ago I became convinced that I have an instinct for fish and fishing. This is not to say that I claim to catch more fish than the average angler or that I fish any better. I simply know where I must fish and I know shortly before I take a fish that I am going to have a rise to the fly I am offering. A lot of people will be amused at this, but people either believe in extra–sensory perception or they don't. I have fished with friends who caught nothing, fished the same flies with the same rod, line and cast in practically the same few feet of water and I have caught fish when they didn't even get a rise. I am told that I am a lucky fisherman. I know lucky fishermen. They are always lucky and repeated luck would seem to be skill, but, without pretending to any false humility, this is not so in my case. I have fished for a long time, nearly all of my life so far, in one place or another, and my skill is only fair. My luck, if you would call it that, is surprising. It is sometimes very bad, but I know both the good and the bad before I put a fly on the water and I am never wrong.

On a good day I have fished for hours without success convinced that I would come to the moment when I would begin to do well. On a bad day I have known that I was doomed to fish without success until I put the rod away again. I have caught fish in places where only instinct suggested a fish might be caught.

There are quite a number of fishermen who will have experienced this sort of thing either at first or second hand. Last summer I had a wonderful example of it when I was in Scotland.

A well-known and skilled salmon fisherman was fishing the local river on which I had been plying a rod for nearly two weeks without success. It rained on my last day and this expert came to fish for a short time on the same water, but he hadn't been there an hour when he decided he must pack up and go by car to a pool on another river where he would take a salmon. He did this. I fished on without success and at night I met the local expert. He had three salmon. He had fished the pool of that other river in company with a dozen other men all spinning with the same sort of spinning gear and the same lures, and he alone had landed salmon. They had all moved along the pool in rotation and according to the rules, and he knew, he insisted, that he would take fish there no matter what the others did or didn't do.

There is something mysterious or mystical, in the business of fishing and it is this that makes it even more fascinating than waiting for duck or walking up birds. The imponderables are legion. The answers are anyone's guess in spite of all the textbooks that have been written. Man, the hunter, isn't born equal. Evolution has almost certainly taken care of those in prehistoric times who lost their sensitivity, their telepathic gifts, their sixth sense. A few people still have these gifts to a varying degree – Kenzie, the gooseman, for instance, who has an apparently fantastic ability to call up hares and bring geese down to within the range of his gun. It makes me smile to read that he acknowledges some gipsy blood. I imagine he would be an accomplished fly-fisherman if he chose to take it up and that he could handle animals equally well.

I remember one September day when, with a companion, I went to fish in a certain Welsh lake. We did very little good during the morning and began to wonder if we shouldn't have chosen the other side of the mountain ridge where there was another lake that had good fish in it. All at once my companion asked me if I had the heart to climb the ridge and walk the five or six miles to that water. I was hot and a little weary, but I saw myself catching a fine trout there and I agreed. We set off. It took us a little more than two hours to climb the ridge and struggle down the long rough slope to the lake we were bound for. When we got there I was even more tired and weary. I put up my rod, put on the fly and went to cast in the particular corner I had chosen. In less than six casts I hooked the finest fish I have ever had from that lake, played and landed it. We caught nothing else. I knew it would be like this before it happened. I knew the fish was there. I had no great trouble with it. It took the fly I knew it would take and its rise was the only rise we saw either before or after I put up my rod, although we both went through the motions of fishing for at least three hours more. It took another two hours to go back over the ridge and it was past ten o'clock at night before we got home. I wish I could have had witnesses!

On another occasion I sat on the shore of one of the largest stretches of water in Wales keeping two friends company. We had fished for hours without persuading a fish to take the flies we offered, although they were rising at The Curse. We began to watch a particular fish that rose in a pattern in a small bay, working its way round in a long elliptical course. I don't think I am given to showing off, but I saw myself casting to this fish and hooking it and bringing it to the net. 'Hold on,' I said, 'watch me catch him. I'll do it right there. He'll rise three times along the shore and I'll take him when he goes out past that rock!' The fish had a considerable way to go. I sat with my rod in my hand, straightened the cast, inspected the fly and when the time came I walked down the shingle, waded out two or three paces, waited for the ripples to subside, cast the fly and hooked the fish. It was the only fish we took all day! I have many flies in my hat and you might say I have a bee in my bonnet, but it really doesn't matter very much. I believe in the sort of fly I fish and to believe is everything. I don't believe I could walk Niagara on a tightrope, blind-folded or not!

Science is something for which I have the greatest respect, even if I know that scientists will laugh at such things as water divining, telepathy, second sight and so on. I tried for a long time to keep my fishing on something like a scientific basis, studying the weather at the time when I caught fish, noting where and how I caught them, the contents of their stomachs and so on. I am ready to admit that my records should have persuaded me that I should fish under the water rather than on the surface. The most artful and probably the most skilled way of fishing for trout is with the nymph. Unfortunately, nymph fishing with most people who go in for it is a rough and ready business without consideration of the facts of entomology and the underwater life of insects that finally emerge to fly. The average wet-fly fisherman's conception of a nymph is something with a hump on its back, a twist of moisture-absorbing wool and three whisks for tails. All cats are grey in the dark.

Wet-flies for lakes may be divided quite simply into things that represent insects and pure and simple lures with the flash of the scales of a small fish. Underwater insects take the form of beetles, larvae and nymphs, the imago about to change its environment for a brief hour in the sun. The exact conditions that lead to the emergence of the hatching fly are the entire answer to both wet and dry-fly fishing except for the use of the well-sunk fly intended to represent the beetle or the somewhat out-sized larvae of the dragonfly. To fish the nymph one needs to know the olive a little better, to be able to recognise it in the nymphal stage, to know the underwater movements of the caddis that finally creeps up a rock and takes off as a sedge. Fishing the rise is easy. It isn't possible to fish the rise when there is no rise.

To anticipate the rise is to anticipate the hatch and to know that requires a degree of perception that so far I haven't been able to claim. I have fished the nymph with varying success. The reason for failure is difficult to diagnose, but given the powers of observation necessary to identify the fly that is hatching one needs to know the form of the nymph that is rising from the bottom and, more important. I think, the way in which it rises.

At a time in my life when I am beginning to think I know how to take a fish by two techniques of fly-fishing, I see before me the whole of the long road once again as I saw it once, I remember, when I watched the larvae of mosquitoes in a rain barrel. How could I ever hope to fish a midge in the right way when midges and mosquito larvae and nymphs moved as they did? The same problem is there if one watches a bloodworm writhing and wriggling to move in the water. How can such movement be attained, not above the water where one has the benefit of refraction, but right in front of the nose of a fish? If colour doesn't matter for objects silhouetted against the sunlit clouds, it may be a very different thing beneath the surface. Fortunately, the nymph and the larvae in most cases are without distinctive colouring. They come in shades of brown and grey. They have to, in order to blend with the bottom and escape the eye of the trout. It isn't so hard to get a passable colouring, but imitation in size, shape and movement are the key to the art. I am inclined to think that my greying beard will be completely white before I am half-way there!

Talking about underwater fishing, which is a more subtle technique, some of the most successful wet-fly fishing done in the welsh lakes is that in which large flies are used, flies that would normally be considered sea-trout size or even small salmon flies. I have often tried this method, but so far the outsize trout it produces have eluded me. It seems to be a question of faith so far as I am concerned. I wonder how deep the fly has gone, is the nylon holding it up and do I need those old-fashioned water-swollen gut casts in order to get as deep as need be? I have difficulty in stopping myself from making a false cast or two to dry the fly and generally speaking it doesn't work for me because I can't concentrate with any conviction that I am going to take a fish, but if I had a lifetime to learn this way and another in which to study nymph-fishing, these are the ways in which I should spend it.

Being a purist has never meant anything to me because purism seems to be a perversion brought about by self-imposed rules. I have fished the dry-fly with the aid of a float more than once, but never simply out of laziness and never to imitate the poacher's otter, for there are much more effective ways of putting flies over the trout than ottering with a bubble and threadline reel. Once, however, I felt compelled to use an oak gall to get a dry fly to fish in a certain pool, and once I used the bubble float and a threadline reel to run a flyaway down through a tunnel of rhododendron bushes. The pool where I used an oak gall is still there, but there are no trout in it now. A few years ago that stream was ruined by cement washings from some hydro-electric work going on a little higher up, but it was a fascinating place when I first knew it and good trout were frequently seen rising on the fringe of a waterfall.

On this occasion the rising fish that attracted my attention was more than good. I tried to reach him, but the breeze kept my fly falling short. When I sought to climb up the rocks round the pool I couldn't get the fly to fall anywhere within range and I was defeated until I thought of using an oak apple. There were oak apples in clusters on the scrub oaks that shaded the pool and I armed myself with one of these, bored a hole right through it and passed my cast through the whole. This gave me a float which I fixed to the cast by pushing a small hard twig into the hole, thus preventing the oak apple from slipping. I then greased the fly heavily, went away above the pool to the brink of the fall, paid out as much line as I thought necessary, dropped the fly and the oak apple on the water and watched them swept over the fall. The oak apple bobbed up and was carried out of the turbulence. The fly came trailing behind and described a long slow arc. It passed exactly over the rising fish. I saw the colour of him as he followed it, away down, perhaps twenty feet below me. When he took it I had no immediate control. I wound up and held him as firmly as I could while I worked my way back down again and finally to the tail of the pool. That he was still on was something of a miracle, perhaps, but he was, and in a little while I had him out. I spent a whole morning taking three fish in this way, but the second two were nothing to be compared with the first.

When I used the bubble and the threadline reel it was to take a fine fat trout that insisted on feeding under bushes in a stream that ran through the grounds of an estate. There were all sorts of obstructions and the bank was dangerously soft, consisting as it did of nothing more than dead leaves compressed into something like peat. I tried hard to get the fly up to the fish and failed utterly. I tried to get it down to him and failed because of low-hanging branches. In the midst of this a wasp alighted on my forehead and stung me under the eyebrow, but I was determined not to be beaten and off I went for the salmon tackle, the small bubble and the spinning reel.

I didn't take long to rig things up, but it was difficult to steer the bubble into the right course. When it trundled slowly away the fly lagged behind and seemed to be going to hang back on the line itself, but by chance the bubble touched an obstruction and the fly was forced to drift away from the line. When it was almost at the fish's station the two were abreast, the fly going as naturally as any living insect riding the current. I watched with great excitement until it seemed that the whole thing had failed because the fish had been looking elsewhere and then there he was, rolling over with the fly in his mouth and the bubble dragging. It took only a second to tighten with a few frantic winds of the handle and the fish, bless him, came upstream no faster than I could wind. I forgot my throbbing eyebrow and the soft bank and down I went to my knees in porridge of leaf-mould and leaves. A bit of sunken twig came with the fish. The line was heavy enough, however, and in a minute or two I had him out.

This success intrigued me so much that I spent two or three days floating flies to fish under bushes, using a bubble half water-logged to keep it at the right speed. There proved to be better fish under the bushes along that stream than any I had caught or seen in the open water. The only drawback turned out to be the hidden snags, the bits of bush and twigs that lay just below the surface. Not everyone could be budged and several times I had to stampede down the bank and retrieve my broken-away bubble or fish it from some branch that held it captive in mid-stream. I hate to think of the fish I never saw simply because I had to plunder into the stream so often, but what wonderful sport I had! Have I mentioned that it rained cats and dogs the whole time, that the place was thick with midges and water ran down my neck as freely as it flowed down the course of the stream?

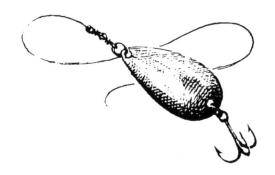

THE HUNGRY PIKE

◇◇

ALTHOUGH I can't deny that of the different branches of sport I have followed I have spent more time fly-fishing than anything else, I have devoted many of my precious days to pike-fishing. At first I was unaware that days were precious. The one thing in which I was really rich was time, and I would come home not by the clock but by the sun, sometimes when darkness had fallen, often when the day had worn away past noon and my lunch was drying up in the oven. For some reason cooks think that a heated-up dish isn't worth having, but then cooks are generally deprived of their appetite by the atmosphere, the heat and fume of the kitchen, while the man who comes home from the field has the hunger of a wolf.

I couldn't even guess at the hours I have spent pike fishing. I am not sure that I want to be told or have the time estimated. Some dreary preacher would surely draw a conclusion about my position in life and how much better off I might have been had I not devoted myself to the futile game of making a pike take a lure.

What is worthwhile in life is for the individual to decide. Society has a self-consciousness about these things that makes judgment worthless. If profit is the yardstick then what did I learn from fishing for pike? I learned what my ancestors weren't here to tell me, something that the hunters of prehistoric times discovered, that the pike is mysterious, snake-like, primeval and secret in its habits and habitat, even although one may see him dozing among the reeds on a hot summer's afternoon, his lithe body barely covered by the water.

All sorts of people dabble at fishing for pike at different times. The pike's presence in the river reduces the salmon angler to the stature of a schoolboy when the salmon won't run up and the pools are stagnant; but merely catching pike doesn't bring the angler within the region of the pike's mystical world, the hidden mystery of his life in the lake or the river throughout the year, year after year, away back to the beginning of things. He is a fish that is widely distributed in both this country, the continent of Europe and North America. He belongs the way the Aryan race belongs and he comes in different forms from the sharp-snouted skinny jack to the great monster with the deep body and gill teeth that could strip the flesh from a man's fingers were he to attempt to lift the fish by the gills after killing him.

Come and see the geds, they said to me long ago when I looked down at a great pool at the bend in the river and down I went to look at the pike that occasionally shot through the lesser fish shoaling on the edge of the reeds. There are faster fish, of course. The pike has only a sudden burst of speed that enables him to overtake his prey. He needs only this. Once he comes up with it the end is certain. Nine times out of ten he takes another fish crosswise in his jaws and then turns it and swallows it head-first, but the tenth time he takes it from the tail and can't let go and I have had this happen often when bringing a small pike in, and have landed two instead of one.

The pike in the river were big enough, but there were bigger pike, I was told, in dozens of quiet water-holes and lakes. Some were big enough to take a child by the arm and drag it into the water. Some could bolt a pheasant or a wild duck that the gunner brought down. There had been one, away over the hills yonder, that had been longer than the keeper who caught it and its tail had dragged on the ground while he carried it home slung over his shoulder. Small boys fished for these monsters with anything they could find for bait. A dead rat from the rickyard, a kitten drowned in the rain-barrel, a frog, a mouse, a bird, a bit of pork, a strip of red flannel, the guts of a chicken. Keepers sometimes used wires fastened to the fence posts and threw out great conger-eel tackle to hold the monsters. People who took them from the river were honour-bound to kill them. A lot of them fed their pike to the hens after boiling them in a setpot or cauldron.

I can't recall that I ever took a pike home. I took perch once, but no one wanted to cook them even though they were as fresh as could be and about half to three quarters of a pound in weight, just above the shoal size normally encountered in the river. Pike, however, were far less welcome. The slime puts everyone off. My grandmother said that pike slime had some healing property, but I never got the chance of asking her exactly what use it could be put to. She died when I was thirteen and took a lot of ancient folklore to the grave with her.

It was a strange thing that although I could have caught some great pike from water that contained giants, I didn't take to pike fishing until I came to Wales, and Wales isn't by any means a pike fisherman's paradise. My first serious excursion was to a lake on the Welsh marches where pike were troubling the keepers of a bird sanctuary. It was an out-of-season invitation. The object of the trip was to destroy pike before they decimated the broods of young duck, and the coarse fishing season didn't apply since the whole enterprise was a private one. I remember this outing in particular because we travelled a considerable distance by car before dawn and stopped once on the way to take rudd from a pond to use them as bait. Fortunately, the rudd were small and ravenous and we had no difficulty in getting all we wanted. I had never before fished for rudd so early in the morning and I have often felt since that they may be more easily caught at daybreak than at any other time. We had collected these fish not to use them as live bait, a method of pike fishing I don't care to use, but in order to spin them as bait on a special tackle.

When we reached the bird sanctuary the keeper welcomed us and took us to the only boat there was – an old waterlogged punt that had been fitted with two rowlocks and two badly-shattered oars. While we rowed we should have been baling. When we stopped to bale out we drifted crabwise towards the trees and the reeds. It seemed at first that we would never be able to win time and distance sufficient to enable us to fish, but when at length we had compromised sufficiently to win the top end of the lake we let the boat drift and hastily baled and made casts. The lake had at one time been a fish stew for an abbey that adjoined the water. It contained bream, some perch and a fair number of pike.

The pike had surely taken their fill of duckling, for while we cast and recast not one made a move in the direction of our

spinners. At noon, when we had grown weary of baling and the water had risen almost to the level of the seats in the old punt, my companion suddenly found a pike had taken and at the same instant a pike took the bait on my side of the punt. We played our fish with great enthusiasm in spite of the fact that the water kept encroaching and by the time I had the gaff in my hand my companion was calling for it to land his fish. Alas, before I could let him have it, he hauled his struggling catch over the edge of the punt and at that moment the tackle parted. The pike began to swim up and down the water-logged punt at a furious pace snapping at our boots and legs and behaving as though it fully intended to take charge of the punt and have us out in the lake.

It didn't help matters when my companion seized the oar and made some desperate stabs at the pike, for it seemed certain to me that soon he would drive a hole in the bottom of our flimsy craft. I slashed away with the gaff every time the pike came within range, but at first this had no effect. The pike was fully aware of the danger and it was amazing to see how he could turn round in such a small area. He swam under the seats and came rushing back again and all the time this went on I couldn't help but feel his teeth would easily rip through my wellingtons. I had once seen two anglers leave a boat to a conger eel they had foolishly brought over the side instead of lashing it to the prow as more experienced anglers would have done, but this was a weedy, peat-bottomed lake and I didn't fancy my chances of swimming ashore.

It was more by luck than anything else that I finally gaffed the swimming fish and hauled it to me to make an end of it by striking it on the head. There was no time left for congratulating each other. We were drifting dangerously under overhanging trees and going down fast. We began to bale out like lunatics and it seemed that we had somehow gone beyond the point of no return until at last the water ceased to lap the seats and we knew we were winning. An hour later we were ashore showing off our catch to the keeper. He had seen our antics in the punt and wondered what we were playing at. He couldn't imagine that two people would fish on and on without baling out. He swore that it seemed to him that we had no freeboard left and were about to go down, but instead of baling we were playing some sort of game. It struck us as being a very funny situation, too – now that our feet were on dry land again. People often say that pike rise or come on the feed at a certain time of day and that this happens all over a particular stretch of water at the same time and sometimes in waters far apart from one another. Our adventure had resulted entirely from this phenomenon and the fact that we shared a gaff instead of carrying one each!

One other odd thing resulted from this episode. We were unloading the car some forty or fifty miles from the lake and three hours or more after catching the pike when one of them, although not the one that had had such fun swimming up and down the punt, came to life and snapped at my hand. This was no mere reflex action, but a positive attempt to bite. I have often found that pike, when their gills are wet and they are not laid where they will dry out and suffocate, are capable of surviving out of water for an unbelievably long period of time. They aren't hard to kill with a priest even if they are more than difficult to hold because of their coating of slime, but they have a wonderful ability to survive and win their way back to the water.

Some time after this episode I was fishing in a lake with extremely boggy banks and, while bringing a pike in, one of my welling tons got sucked off. I hastily drew the fish up through the rushes and back into the long grass while I went back to recover my boot. When I had restored the boot to my peat-blackened leg I went in search of the pike. It had broken free of the tackle and I couldn't find it anywhere. It was a fish of something round six or seven pounds in weight, but of course it blended well with the grass. I searched in vain and then gave up and resumed fishing farther along the bank. Four or five hours later, coming that way again I looked down and there was the pike, his eyes looking balefully up at me as he lay deep in the grass perhaps twenty feet from the place where I had left him. He was apparently not a bit the worse for having been out of the water so long. No doubt the moss and damp grass had helped him to survive and he could probably have been transported in a covering of these things much more safely than in a small tank of water.

Talking of the pike's coming on to feed reminds me of an occasion when I was fishing in Scotland a few years ago. They had told me that I might get large trout from a certain piece of water, but I had no hope of reaching out to them with fly tackle and I had better spin. Accordingly I set up spinning tackle and waded away down through a marsh, leaving most of the remainder of my gear in the brake I was using. My first cast in this stretch of water produced an immediate rise to the little rubber spinning bait I was using, but instead of a large trout it soon became obvious from the sinuous movement and the general behaviour of the fish that I had a pike on. I played him and shouted as loudly as I could for the gaff, remembering that I had only four-pound nylon and no trace that would stand the sawing of a large pike's teeth.

My son came struggling down with the gaff, but at the moment he reached me and I held out my hand for it the pike broke my tackle and swam into the reeds. He was, I judged, a big fish for that water. I put on an almost identical rubber bait and cast out in exactly the same place and as soon as the bait dropped a fish took it. I played this second fish and brought it to the gaff. It was identical in size to the first. It might indeed have been that first fish supposing it had shaken the rubber lure from its jaw, but when I landed it there was no sign of the fish having been hooked before. These two fish are or were the largest pike I had ever caught, or should I say, nearly caught? I am convinced that they were two fish and not one trying to make amends for his previous failure to commit suicide.

Catching the same fish twice at successive casts isn't beyond many a pike angler's experience, of course, and I may have been mistaken. I have caught the same pike or at least hooked the same pike twice. Once when I used to go to spin at a lake up in the hills not many miles from where I now live, I had the habit of making my own minnows and fastening the hooks with a soft wire. Late one Saturday evening, spinning one of these minnows and hoping for a good perch I took a pike that came right to my feet. A week later, fishing in the same place, I hooked a pike and brought him to the gaff. Fast in his jaw was the remainder of my minnow from the previous week's encounter. He hadn't worked

152

it out of his skin and I removed it and restored it to my tackle box none the worse for having been taken round the lake a good few times during the week.

It was in a lake near this one that I hooked ten pike at ten casts one bright afternoon in late summer, the fishing beginning and ending quite abruptly. That trout rise and stop rising unaccountably everyone knows and the same impulse takes pike even if they aren't stimulated simply by hatching flies. This afternoon everything happened to be right. I sniffed the air and it seemed to me to be just right for catching a pike. The breeze was cool, but the water was a little cooler than the air. The clouds were high and far off. There was just the faintest suggestion of autumn about that day. Away on the lower fields the corn was ripe and they had been opening roads for the binder. The rowans were rusted at the edges. The berries were a brilliant red.

I began to fish and no pike moved for the first hour and then all at once I had one on. I brought him in and killed him, for this was a duck lake and a condition of my fishing permit was that I should destroy the pike I caught. I cast again as soon as I had killed the fish and at once another pike took me. At the tenth cast I hooked my tenth pike. They were all identical in size, little more than jack. I weighed one of them. He was exactly four and a half pounds. Perhaps breaking off to do this also broke the spell. I fished steadily on all afternoon and well into the late evening without touching another fish. I didn't take the last one in the lake either, because I fished there a good many times after that and took my share of pike, although never again successively and never as many as ten even in a whole afternoon.

It was on this same little reed-fringed lake that I went to fish with a friend who had never fished for pike before. Apart from my spinning tackle all I could offer him were two pike floats, a rod, reel and line and a hook for use with live-bait. In order to set him up to fish I explained how to rig the live-bait and went again to spin a small spoon in order to take a perch so that he might have his bait. When I came back with the small perch my friend settled down to watch his floats. I had told him not to strike if the first float began to move or went down, but when the second float followed the first he should lift the rod and set the hook. By this time the pike would have moved the perch round in his jaw and gorged him. My friend nodded and I left him to the business while I began to spin.

I had just taken my first fish when I was accosted by the livebaiter. What should he do? The first float had gone down, but the second hadn't followed it and now the first float was going off merrily on its own. It seemed that he had made a poor knot somewhere and the knot had parted between the floats. I couldn't understand why he had had to make a knot, but I was concerned to retrieve my tackle if I could and I hurried along the bank with my spinning rod in my hand to see the pike float bobbing out about as far as I could hope to cast. There was nothing for it but to try to catch the line beyond the float with the treble hook of my spinner, and after about four casts this happened. The treble hook slid up the line and lodged in the cork of the float and by some miracle the line with the pike on the end didn't slip out of the float and I was able to play the fish on this link. After about five minutes I brought him in and gaffed him. It seemed to me that I had pulled off a hundred to one chance. The pike had been well-hooked, but the line held only because a poor knot prevented it slipping through the stem of the float.

How are the really big pike caught? Experts agree, I think, that live-baiting has the edge on all other methods. It cannot be denied that the best bait for the biggest trout is another trout, or a dace or a minnow and these fished alive are a certain attraction for a fish that is already a predator without having earned the colourful name of cannibal. In the case of pike which are the hawks of the shoals, the vultures of the riverbed, the eagles that stoop to kill the lesser sorts of fish, the live-bait method is the soundest of all if the fisherman happens to want a specimen fish. Some people say that the fins of a perch should be trimmed to encourage the pike to take this lesser fish as a bait since the dorsal fin when set acts as a protection for the perch. I am not at all sure that the dorsal fin being erected has anything to do with discouraging the enemy of the perch. I am inclined to think that the perch elevates his dorsal fin to display or intimidate his rivals. A pike can crush much more formidable things than the spines the perch carries.

The perch is a good enough bait, but the pike, I think, prefers a rudd, a roach or a dace. He will take a small trout or even a minnow or a miller's thumb if these can be anchored in his beat. He will also take dead baits of different kinds, such as a herring, but live-bait has movement and nothing can attract quite so easily as a fish tied to a particular place and struggling to get free. The outstanding pike of recent years seem to have been taken in the main on live-bait and not a few of these live-bait rigs are still equipped with more hooks than a ship's chandlers and resemble the old-fashioned and now illegal gorge tackle so much favoured half a century ago.

Never having had much liking for live-baiting I have never put the systems to the test. I prefer to lure my fish. I cannot deny that I see the advantage of a worm for bottom-feeding trout and I would use a dead bait for a pike, but for sport and simplicity I think a good lure takes a lot of beating. Not every day will the pike move out to follow a lure while he can hardly resist the movement of a dead or dying fish since part of his job is to clear the river of its corpses, but a lure requires a certain skill in presentation while a live-bait is something that waits for the fish like a poacher's set line and has no more merit so far as I am concerned. It doesn't matter who puts out a live-bait or who wheels it in again with the fish well-hooked away down in the stomach, but it does matter who works a lure in a lake or river.

Talking about live-baiting reminds me of the experience of a friend some years ago. He was fishing a small rudd for a pike which he hoped to take from a private lake. The tackle had been set up for some time and had been periodically examined to see that the bait was still alive and working, but nothing had happened and my friend settled down on the bank to have a nap. Perhaps half an hour had passed when he thought to look at the floats again. They seemed all right except for the fact that near them a swan was investigating below the surface with its rear end in the air. My friend thought no more of this although he wondered if there would be any chance of the pike coming at the bait so long as the swan hung about.

Some little time passed and my friend looked again. By a coincidence, it seemed, the swan was still in the same position. He watched it for several seconds before it occurred to him to wind in his tackle, whereupon he discovered that the swan had swallowed the tethered rudd! Now somehow or other the swan must have been getting air, perhaps by dragging its head above water at intervals but as soon as my friend began to reel in the swan began to fight and flap. To break the tackle off would have been no solution. The weight to which the rudd had been anchored was enough to drown the swan, so there was nothing else for it but to play the poor swan until he gave up and came ashore. This was done, but alas the swan was deeply hooked in the throat and had to be destroyed, a tragedy which for me underlines the folly of setting lines or leaving tackle to fish unwatched.

Perhaps the last word in baiting for pike should be an account of a giant pike taken by a river keeper on a certain river in Scotland two winters ago. This monster had been offered a variety of baits from set lines. He had straightened some very large hooks and broken several thicknesses of snare wire used to tether the line. At last the local smith was induced to forge a special hook. Some heavy wire was used to fasten the line to a stake in the bank and the special hook was baited with a collie pup. The great pike rose in the night and swallowed the pup and was there the following morning to be hauled out and killed. He was the biggest pike seen in that or any other river in the locality in living memory and nothing else, positively nothing else, could have held him or lured him!

The biggest pike hasn't been recorded yet, I fancy, but the biggest pike in legend is probably a fish said to have been taken in the days of Charles Cotton near Newport. It weighed 'upwards of 170lb.' Mr Frank Buckland, the naturalist, is said to have been given a pike that weighed 100lb. and came from Whittlesea Mere. The legendary Loch Ken pike was something of this order and I believe that somewhere in Scotland there is a skull said to confirm the size of the Loch Ken monster. Here in Wales the pike legend is no less prevalent than elsewhere and the story tells of a pike that took a horse by the nose and drowned it. This same giant drowned a child which it seized by the hand. Perhaps it lived in Tegid, the lake of legend.

Outside legend and authenticated is the famous Lough Conn pike taken by John Garvin in 1920, and on the spoon at that. It weighed 53lb. There are still great pike in Ireland, many to be had in Scotland and not a few lurking in the waters of the Fenland where Jim Vincent fished his big spoons. For my own part I can lay no claim to having caught big pike. They have persistently eluded me. Perhaps I have never been single-minded enough to succeed. It takes a tired man to sing a tired song, but it takes a more than eager fanatic to take a record fish. There have been winters during which, had circumstances presented themselves, I had it in mind to put away the gun for a season at least and try to catch a big pike. Unfortunately, this invariably meant travelling a long way. The acid waters and the nature of many places in North Wales are such that big pike here are middling fish elsewhere and the dream has been put away as the years have gone on. Once I could have had my big pike.

Once they showed in the river or swirled in the lochs of the country in which I was brought up. Loch Lomond itself wasn't too far away, but my parents didn't suspect that I might have this ambition dormant within me and they moved away too soon. The great geds that the village urchins hooked and hauled out were big enough, of course, but I knew well that there were bigger fish below the water, great monsters that had been spawned by great monsters, ad infinitum back to the first water and the first dawn. It is better, perhaps, to cherish an illusion than to have it disintegrate in the light of experience. When I fish for pike now, sometimes in a summer when I visit my old haunts in the north, I never fish for the legend but only for the sort of fish that takes my lure.

LOOKING BOTH WAYS

<><><><><><><><><><><><><><><><><><><><><><><><><><><><><><><>

THERE are unfortunately no standards by which we can compare our delight in things. While for one man a morning on the marsh may mean a forbidding vista of mud and drunken, weed-draped fences, for another it holds the magic of the opening day, the distant sound of conversing water-birds, the sight of towering clouds and a fantasy of colour radiating from the still-hidden sun. We all react differently to circumstances and what matters is that we enjoy what we choose to do.

I have had my days of wretchedness plodding through mud and morass wet to the skin, but my experience nevertheless has been almost sustained delight. Looking back is not only pleasant, it encourages one to travel hopefully and it brings home to us the significance of change. What changes there have been even since my boyhood! It isn't so long ago that the greater part of the countryside had that wonderful remoteness, that shut-off isolation, that peace one knew passing through tall, hushed woods that brooded over deserted roads, or when one saw the sleeping lodges of great estates behind white-painted gates. Journeys progressed at the right pace, even if beyond the hills, away in the towns, people were beginning to hurry for no reason except that their neighbour was apparently hurrying, too.

In the quiet countryside this was still the day of the gig and the trotting pony and if the motor-car penetrated so far into the wilderness it left a sweet, sickly odour of petrol that hung in the air long after it had gone. Estate workers went their leisurely way. Wood-smoke ascended from the chimneys of stone cottages and undisciplined hens flew up on to roadside walls, roosted in trees and laid away in nettle beds. When the estate shoots were held it wasn't hard to find beaters. The countryside was well-populated by ploughboys, ditchers, thatchers, stockmen, joiners, smiths and carters. Every keeper had his helpers and his apprentice lad who was promised a suit of tweeds and a better job than merely carrying a bag of hares. The colour of this world was richer because of the men and women who peopled it, men with straps at their knees and women in long skirts who picked potatoes and stopped to watch the guns going down the last few yards of the rootfield with the keepers and their pied spaniels in attendance.

How often one would find this picture repeated in different places across the autumn fields of yesterday, see the driven birds topping the tallest trees or the game cart drawn by a fat-bellied cob coming back out of the silent moor. Yesterday they had hare shoots where they made such bags as brought dismay to the hearts of the keepers and their helpers alike, yet they didn't exterminate the brown hare any more than they exterminated mallard or teal or wintering fowl from the north. It seems to me that the geese of yesterday really did fly lower and that the hares were as thick as the fleas on an old hedgehog. The woods held even greater multitudes of pigeons perhaps because the woods were more sacred than they are today. There were more painted cock pheasants lording it over greater companies of hens, of course, because breeding and rearing were much more widespread and there were keepers who didn't question the fairness of day that began at first light and continued until the last coop had been closed and bats were flying.

There never will be such days again, the old men say. The same old men insist that the ale they drank long ago was stronger, better, cheaper and all things today are inferior. The winters were colder and the summers were a blaze of glory. The long ago water meadows swarmed with mallard, wigeon, teal and snipe. When someone walking the water-logged hollow put up a cock pheasant from the fringe of the alders (cock pheasants have always loved trees in swampy ground) a hundred – no, two hundred duck took the air, some paddling and splashing off the pools and some springing straight up to climb into the mist in the manner of the handsome little teal. The man with the gun was speechless with admiration of it all and not dismayed to think that he might never see such a sight again, for he knew that the chances were that in the next meadow, down at the bend of the river, in the forest of swaying reeds, it would happen again and he would flush as many fowl or even more.

Are the old men wrong and do they only remember their finest summers, their brightest autumn mornings, their breathtaking days in the frost of winter? The records seem to substantiate their sad, nostalgic story. The changes of this century are perhaps more of a chain reaction than anything with which they might have been compared in the day of Colonel Hawker. All at once

we were rebuilding roads, designing machinery, uprooting men, speeding the tempo of life because world wars were speeding men to confront one another with guns. In a short space of time the new invention became obsolete. In the fields the carter, the ploughman and the keeper's boy had left; the binder was made obsolete by the combine harvester. The farmer's sons and their helpers no longer made hay with hand rakes and watched the young partridges stealing over the bank. The green grass was cut for silage or the ripe hay was cut in a day and pounded into bales, the hayfield left as shorn as a newly-fleeced ewe. All at once we knew the difference between one age and another!

No one can stay progress and the things it entails. No one can immediately say what is entirely good or bad when the wheels are still turning. The strong ale our grandfathers drank when they came from the field and put away their fowling pieces isn't to be had at any price. Hodge is long since out of his smock and his forelock has been trimmed. He plays darts and drinks a brew that comes from a metal drum, impregnated with a squirt of carbon dioxide to give it lift and pass as English beer. It is no wonder that a large number of dallying sportsmen, thinking about yesterday, find themselves isolated, cut off like a fowler far out on a strange marsh without a marker. It is time to think about tomorrow because the shrinking field, although it shrinks almost imperceptibly, shrinks continually, day by day, bisected by a motorway wider than any Roman military road by many yards, encroached upon by plateaux of concrete, cooling towers, generating plants, atomic piles.

All the while more men come to fish, to find a few acres of rough shooting, a corner in the marsh where they may sport themselves as their ancestors did. The problems created are immense and not least among them is that of conservation of our resources and the intelligent training of the young. It is said again and again that it befits the serious shooting man to see that what is best in sporting ethics is passed on and what is reprehensible is put away. I am inclined to think that we must be careful not to condemn Tom, Dick and Harry without having done something towards their general enlightenment and education.

What are known as 'shore cowboys' are mainly a post-war phenomenon. They shoot badly and do untold harm to wild life, they mutilate and they endanger life and limb without being aware of their colossal ignorance. The law may take account of this irresponsible behaviour, but it doesn't punish as often as it might for lack of evidence or precise information. Even if it did the problem isn't simply one of bringing delinquents to book.

It is hard to contrive that sporting guns be sold only to responsible individuals and perhaps impossible to insist that those who buy guns be sponsored, yet we are all aware that a twelve-bore is a much more lethal weapon than a ·22 rifle, for which a firearms certificate is required. Someone, somewhere, will one day frame legislation that will put some of our mistakes right, but in the meantime every shooting man must be sure that he has brainwashed his own offspring until he points his gun at no one, unloads it when crossing hedges or fences, and shoots only where he can see things he may lawfully shoot. Conservation is a word that some people take to themselves, implying a kind of patent right, a Sabbatarian smugness notwithstanding. It seems to me that the unorganised shooting man will be pilloried and misrepresented so long as he ignores the signs that mark the way ahead.

There is a moral to be drawn from the facts surrounding the protection of the barnacle goose. It may be overlooked that wildfowlers co-operated to the full in this business and some of them are cynically aware that there is small chance of this goose ever being removed from the list of protected birds, though it rises from the shore like midges over a waterhole. Few fowlers doubt that the barnacles will become a nuisance to the farmer and that to quieten their outcry and demands for compensation something will have to be done, if not in the next year or two, then in five or six years, perhaps. The remedy is almost certain to be the appointment of conservancy officers specially delegated to reduce the barnacle goose to reasonable proportions. The logic here lies in the fact that control itself will be governed by such means.

If some other species of fowl comes near the danger mark and the same result becomes inevitable, it will surely be through the short-sightedness of wildfowlers in not recognising the signs.

It is only the grasshopper mind that doesn't consider tomorrow. I am sure that the majority of responsible sportsmen are concerned about the future, but I wonder if they often take the trouble to impress their opinions on the happy-go-lucky fellows with that fatal opportunist philosophy? I am afraid they hardly ever even try.

Pessimism isn't something that infects the man who loves the field for very long. It never rains for long, the sun comes out sooner or later and after the darkest hour comes the day. Not long ago I crouched in a creek waiting for the morning flight with a companion who was some years my junior. We talked about things as I had known them, compared them with my companion's experience and speculated about the day when his two-year-old son would have graduated to manhood and the opportunity to flight. Would there even be a flight? Some people paint a very dreary daybreak, a grim tomorrow and the future isn't discernible even in the atomic age, but I am pretty sure that geese will flight as the sun rises and sets, hares will run the hills, unless the whole canopy of heaven is obscured by a roof under which the farmer raises baby beef and hothouse swedes, and sportsmen will await the flight and walk the field. All this will go on even in an age when the town absorbs more and more of the countryside and its inhabitants, providing the sportsman is jealous of his reputation, does nothing to bring shame on himself and meets emotional attack with logic and fact.

Also published by Merlin Unwin Books

The Poacher's Handbook by Ian Niall £14.95

The Poacher's Cookbook by Prue Coats £11.99

The Countryman's Bedside Book by BB £18.95

The Naturalist's Bedside Book by BB £17.99

The Shootingman's Bedside Book by BB £18.95

The Fisherman's Bedside Book by BB £18.95

The Best of BB by BB £18.95

Moonlighting by Michael Brown £15.99

A Countryman's Creel by Conor Farrington £14.99

Fishing with Harry by Tony Baw £15.99

The Sporting Gun's Bedside Companion
by Douglas Butler £15.99

Private Thoughts from a Small Shoot
by Laurence Catlow £17.99